THE OPENING OF T

The so-called Third Eye is
release psychic powers and
in new directions. Dr Bake.
techniques for arousing its powers.

The Magnetic Aura of the Master

THE OPENING OF THE THIRD EYE

by

Dr DOUGLAS BAKER
B.A., M.R.C.S., L.R.C.P., F.Z.S.

THE AQUARIAN PRESS
Wellingborough, Northamptonshire

This Edition 1977
Ninth Impression 1985

ISBN 0 85030 140 8

Printed and bound in Great Britain

Contents

Part One
THE TRUE NATURE OF MATTER

1

The Mystery of Man's Mind

The trials and struggles of man on the path are immense. History and mythology are full of allusions to it. Jason and the Golden Fleece, the Knights of the Holy Grail, Hercules and his Twelve Labours, the separating of the Goats from the Sheep, are but a few that we have derived from the Western cultures. In the East, the best known allusion to the struggle for Initiation is that of Arjuna on the Battlefield, as described in the 'Song Celestial', the *Bhagavad Gita*.

We no sooner begin to accept the basic propositions of Ancient Wisdom concerning the inner reality of Man's Soul, when we are immediately confronted with immense new concepts, the encompassing of which places heavier and heavier burdens on the mind and calls for even greater occult disciplines.

Here are some of the prodigious concepts we must face:

1. That the material world is an ILLUSION.
2. That TIME can be manipulated, slowed down, so that we can live in the ETERNAL NOW.
3. That we have a divine SELF ... a higher nature ... the real inner entity or soul WHICH WE CANNOT EVEN REMEMBER and Who ignores the petty problems of our personalities.
4. That we, our lower selves, are asleep or, at the best, only partly conscious.
5. That we have powers LATENT WITHIN us.
6. That the ultimate, for us, is immortality and eternity.

And there are many, many others, equally complex.

It is hard work reaching even a vague understanding of what these concepts imply, and that HARD WORK constitutes the struggles of THE PATH because we have to do that work and make those struggles whilst still living in the world of the personality. Few personalities can cope with the normal demands and stress of life let alone those of SIX MORE INNER WORLDS.

Knowledge and understanding of the higher worlds are hard to come by. The three traditional paths to self-unfoldment are:

1. Service to mankind.
2. Focus of the Mind and
3. Meditation.

There are other ways but they are not safe and their rewards are as illusory as matter itself.

We do not easily comprehend the Inner Worlds or the life of those worlds because they exist, as it were, in different dimensions from those for which we possess cognitive faculties which we call the five senses.

Elsewhere I have dealt extensively with some of the powers latent in man. Here I am more concerned with the concepts of MAYA and NEW DIMENSIONS as keys to the mystery of man's mind. If we study the Ancient Wisdom with care, we find references everywhere to the illusory nature of the material world and these cannot be sidetracked. We are told that our cities, our homes, our furniture and even our loved possessions like brothers and sisters, parents or children, are all forms of deception.

Fragments of Reality
Even our own physical bodies are mutable, ever-changing, impermanent shadows of the truth.

The occult proposition goes even further. Even the astral body is a shell, an illusion that must fade, useful for experiencing the astral world and moving about in, but still an ILLUSION! The mental body is equally illusory. It interpenetrates and lives in the world of mental substance. The worlds of the personality, the PHYSICAL, ASTRAL and MENTAL, are an illusion, or Maya.

Plato says it; Blavatsky says it; ancient Hindu and Chinese traditions teach it; Ouspensky, Gurdjieff, Besant, Leadbeater and Bailey.

Even Einstein, in his way, says it.

And SCIENCE is of no help to us any more in denying it. For a long time it clung to the concept of matter being made up of tiny particles ... atoms. Later, it was accepted that the atoms were themselves made up of fundamental particles like protons and electrons. But they were anything but fundamental!

The quantum theory of the 1920's showed that atoms made a coherent mathematical pattern but the fundamental particles could no longer be treated as separate, individual objects, but only as STATISTICAL EFFECTS.

> All that one can say about an electron is that there are definite odds that it will be in a particular place at a particular time. It was turned from a thing into A KIND OF BLUR, which behaved as a 'particle' one moment when observed in one way, and as a 'wave' when observed in another.*

But this was exactly what theosophists and others had been saying fifty years earlier.

The electrons form shells in the atom only in the sense that these non-existent particles are in rapid movement about their nucleus, which might be protons and neutrons, but even for the latter, little hope is held out that they are anything more than agglomerations of energy patterns.

Emptiness of the Atom

Then there is the extraordinary emptiness of the atom. When we go chasing for the tangible part of the atom we find practically nothing there!

If we expanded a hydrogen atom to the size of a cathedral, its electron would perhaps be the size of a nickel! The nucleus

---

* John Davy in *The Observer*, February 1970: 'Do We Or Don't We Understand The Secret Of Life?'

might be merely a single priest in the cathedral. The rest of the atom is empty. There would be plenty of room say for particles the size of a grain of sand (astral) or even smaller (mental). In the case of gold there would merely be more priests and nickels ...

Even when we come to a piece of iron, we have to admit that it is merely a confinement of rapidly moving iron molecules ... rapidly moving atoms ... empty atoms! ... rushing about in all directions, giving us the impression or illusion of a solid.

Apply heat energy to the block of iron: the atoms move faster and the block gets bigger (expands) and then the iron changes its state, melts, and we have a liquid. Pour heat into the liquid and it changes its state again into gas. Everything about us is but empty atoms in one of these states.

It is the MOTION of the atoms which makes us apprehend water one moment as ICE and another moment as the liquid ... and as a vapour, etc. We forget this as we work with materials ... that their MOTION as well as their inner motions decide how we understand them with our senses. Our senses can't tell us continuously that the atoms are empty, that their 'tangible' parts are but 'blurs of energy' or vortices of energy, as the occultist has always described the atom since he first symbolised its motion with the ancient and sacred symbol of the swastika. Our minds have to tell us that their servants, the senses, are fooling us, and have fooled us for many ages.

To all the above, scientific, or non-scientific, the Secret Doctrine says Amen!

Slayer of the Real

But the mind is as much a slayer of the real as its senses, for it is hardly able to see things more clearly than them. It, too, is restricted to the world of three dimensions, when there are other dimensions in which Man's real nature exists ... what is known in occultism as the **noumenal** world.

At least, we are learning here that things are not what they seem to be.

Today we accept the proposition of Einstein and his equation:

$$E = M C^2$$

which in the end means that matter and energy are interchangeable.

The Wisdom of the Ages has always said that ALL IS ENERGY AND VIBRATION. When energy manifests as matter it produces illusion or Maya. Matter is a VERY TEMPORARY FOCAL POINT for energy and that goes for all forms. But underlying all forms there is an energy pattern at a higher level constantly pulling matter into it. This is the real, enduring nature of a phenomenon ... that which we call the **noumen.**

The energy of mind and emotions is interchangeable with the densest objects. The mind of a blessing priest impregnates and becomes part of the water he blesses.

Can one penetrate the densest object with the energy of mind? Occultists say it can be done. The phenomena of thought transference or telepathy and of hypnotism involves just this. The samadhi of the yogi is but the realization that all is one ... Life links all material form and uses the form to express itself. It is the life essence which is important, not the form.

Occultists always see everything in terms of vibration, including that of one's own body, which has a NOTE! The note of the solar logos is said to be AUM.

And what if all of animated nature
Be but organic harps, diversely framed,
That tremble into thought, as o'er them sweeps
Plastic and vast, one intelligible breeze,
At once the soul of each, and God of ALL?

Samuel T. Coleridge

Within us is a noumenal form or soul that works through a phenomenal body made of matter of the material world ... which has no real existence at all. It is an emptiness and nothingness without the energy transformer of the over-shadowing soul ... and we love that body and the material world in which it thrives ... that material world that enmeshes us ... ensnares us ... surrounds us with a veil of glamour and diverts our attention from our real being.

'But now in some mysterious
fashion
time was changed,
and time speeded up,
so that I saw generations
of birds ...'

J.B. Priestley's Dream-vision

J.B. Priestley dreamed the following after helping with bird-ringing at St Catherine's lighthouse on the Isle of Wight.

I dreamt I was standing at the top of a very high tower, alone, looking down upon myriads of birds all flying in one direction; every kind of bird was there, all the birds in the world. It was a noble sight, this vast aerial river of birds. But now in some mysterious fashion the gear was changed, and time speeded up, so that I saw generations of birds, watched them break their shells, flutter into life, weaken, falter and die. Wings grew only to crumble; bodies were sleek and then, in a flash, bled and shrivelled; and death struck everywhere and at every second. What was the use of all this blind struggle towards life, this eager trying of wings, all this gigantic meaningless biological effort? As I stared down, seeming to see every creature's ignoble little history almost at a glance, I felt sick at heart. It would be better if not one of them, not one of us at all, had been born, if the struggle ceased for ever. I stood on my tower, still alone, desperately unhappy, but now the gear was changed again and time went faster still, and it was rushing by at such a rate, that the birds could not show any movement but were like an enormous plain sown with feathers. But along this plain, flickering through the bodies themselves, there now passed a sort of white flame, trembling, dancing, then hurrying on; and as soon as I saw it I knew this flame was life itself, the very quintessence of being; and then it came to me, in a rocket-burst of ecstasy, that nothing mattered, nothing could ever matter, because nothing else was real, but this quivering, hurrying lambency of being. Birds, men or creatures not yet shaped and coloured, all were of no account except so far as this flame of life travelled through them. It left nothing to mourn over behind it; what I had thought of as tragedy was mere emptiness of a shadow show, for now all real feeling was caught and purified and danced on ecstatically with the white flame of life. I had never felt before such deep happiness as I knew at the end of my dream of the tower and the birds ...

2

New States of Awareness

At one end of man's consciousness we have that upon which his senses dwell ... a vast miasma of illusion. At the other end is his brain, through which he must interpret what the senses tell him.

We know practically nothing about the human brain. We cannot say, in terms of brain tissue, what produces its four main functions:

INTELLIGENCE
MEMORY
INSTINCT and
CHARACTER

WE DO KNOW THAT THE SENSES CAN FOOL THE BRAIN and there are many examples of this. Most of us think that the brain SEES, and HEARS, and FEELS, and SMELLS and TASTES, but it doesn't really. Smell doesn't come in contact with the brain cells that give us information about it. In the final stage of sensory perception all impulses, whether they are smell or sight or hearing or any other, reach the brain as currents of electricity and the surface of the brain sorts them out.

We don't actually see ... electrical impulses triggered off by the presence of light tell us this fact. Our senses tell us a few facts about our environment in terms of three dimensions of space. We 'see' only a few facets of the truth. We lack the capacity to interpret any more because we will not allow our real natures to get to grips with them.

We are but embryos ... physically, emotionally, mentally and especially spiritually. We still are half formed and have many new organs to build. New organs of perception have yet

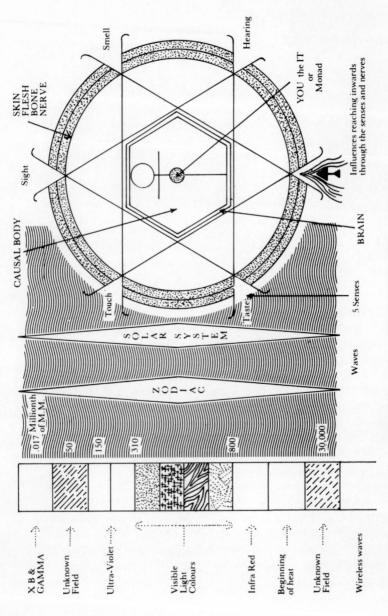

THE ELECTRO-MAGNETIC SPECTRUM
with man's deficient sensory equipment immersed within it.

to manifest or to come out of dormancy ...

A pineal gland, now atrophied ...

Chakrams in the head and heart regions ...

A lens to be built into the aura in front of the forehead.

The Three Blind Hindus

We are interpreting only a fraction of the truth. We are like the three blind Hindus, blind since birth, who were led to an elephant. One felt its tusk and said it was a spear. One felt its tail and said it was a rope and the third felt its body and said it was a wall. The truth was far beyond this ... We in our turn see very little of the truth ... we pool our few experiences of it and trust to clairvoyants, seers and mystics for the rest ... but we are still very much like the three blind Hindus in this respect. And in the end we need the spiritual eye of inner vision to see the truth (or the elephant) as a whole ... an eye that takes many lives of rebirth on this planet to unfold or must be opened through intense disciplines and sacrifice which we call YOGA.

We are much like an insect in metamorphosis ... our body parts and equipment must grow and change to give us new states of awareness and mastery of our environment.

At first we are an embryo, blind within the egg of Maya or illusion. Later, as the hatched caterpillar we have two-dimensional perception and an acquisitiveness for material things (only the green leaf interests the caterpillar).

Later, we must withdraw into pupation like the yogi withdraws from the world and immense reconstruction of our inner and outer framework leads to our emancipation from the pupal case, the yogi in samadhi ... and as the free imago we soar into new dimensions of space like the gloriously winged butterfly of the orchard.

We need to perceive new dimensions. But first let us look at the occult teachings on the nature of that which enslaves us, the material world and its building bricks, the ultimate physical particle. (The brain will see only what the mind wills it to see. In hypnotism, the brain of the one hypnotized will see what the mind of the hypnotist orders it to see).

There are none so blind as those who will not see!

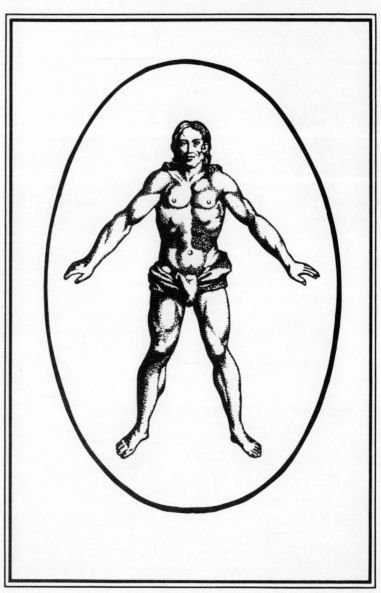

Man Within His Auric Egg

A BUTTERFLY

by G. Eustace Owen

from *Children's Greater World*

A butterfly rested upon a flower,
  Gay was he and light as a flake,
And there he met a caterpillar
  Sobbing as though his heart would break;
It hurt the happy butterfly
  To see a caterpillar cry.

Said he, 'Whatever is the matter?
  And may I help in any way?'
'I've lost my brother,' wept the other,
  'He's been unwell for many a day;
Now I discover, sad to tell,
  He's only a dead and empty shell.'

'Unhappy grub, be done with weeping,
  Your sickly brother is not dead;
His body's stronger and no longer
  Crawls like a worm, but flies instead.
He dances through the sunny hours
  And drinks sweet nectar from the flowers'.

'Away, away deceitful villain,
  Go to the winds where you belong.
I won't be grieving at your leaving,
  So take away your lying tongue.
Am I a foolish slug or snail,
  To swallow such a fairy tale?'

'I'll prove my words, you unbeliever,
  Now listen well, and look at me.
I am none other than your brother,
  Alive and well and fancy free.
Soon you'll be with me in the skies
  Among the flirting butterflies.'

'Ah!' cried the mournful caterpillar,
  ''Tis clear I must be seeing things.
You're only a spectre sipping nectar,
  Flicking your ornamental wings,
And talking nonsense by the yard.
  I will not hear another word.'

The butterfly gave up the struggle.
  'I have,' he said, 'no more to say.'
He spread his splendid wings and ascended
  Into the air and flew away.
And while he fluttered far and wide,
  The caterpillar sat and cried.

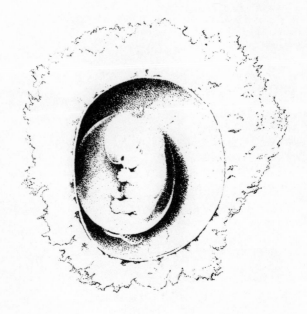

We are but embryos ... physically, emotionally, mentally and especially spiritually.

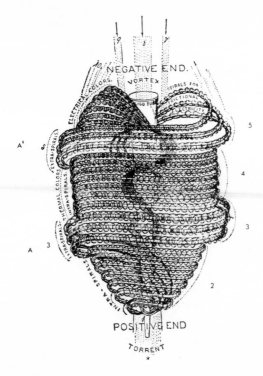

EHTERICO-ATOMIC PHILOSOPHY OF FORCE

The general form of the atom, including the spirals and 1st spirillae, together with influx and efflux ethers, represented by dots, which pass through these spirillae. The 2nd and 3rd spirillae with their still finer ethers are not shown.

(From *The Principles of Light and Color* Edwin D. Babbitt, New York, 1878).

The Ultimate Particle of Matter

Whilst today science is only just beginning to talk of electrons and other atomic particles as 'blurs of energy' rather than solid structures, in 1878 Edwin Babbitt had already shown, in his remarkable book, *The Principles of Light and Color* the whirling energy-vortex which is the ultimate atom or ANU as it is called by Theosophy. Later C.W. Leadbeater and Annie Besant were able to confirm, almost exactly Babbitt's description and drawing (see opposite). Later, Geoffrey Hodson, the Theosophical clairvoyant was able to confirm that the anu corresponded to the electron.

Anu appear and disappear, welling up, as it were from the astral plane, and disappearing from the physical on to the astral again.

DESCRIPTION OF THE ANU

It is a living heart, pulsating with energy; with its three thicker whorls and the seven thinner, it is also a transformer, each whorl is made up of seven orders of spirillae. Spirals and spirillae are the basis of its structure and the anu is fashioned to do a work. In the three whorls flow currents of different electricities, the seven vibrate in response to etheric waves of all kinds ... to sounds, light, heat, etc.; they show the seven colours of the spectrum; give out the seven sounds of the natural scale; respond in a variety of ways to physical vibration ... flashing, singing, pulsing bodies, they move incessantly, inconceivably beautiful and brilliant.

The atom or anu has, as observed so far, three proper motions, i.e. motions on its own, independent of any imposed on it from outside. It turns incessantly upon its own axis, spinning like a top: It describes a small circle with its axis, as though the axis of the spinning top moved in a small circle (nutation): It has a regular pulsation, a contraction and expansion like the pulsation of a heart (with each diastole it fills with energy through the vortex; and with each systole pours a torrent of energy from its south pole ... the energy of prana, the life force). When a force is brought to bear upon it, it dances up and down, flings itself wildly from side to side, performs the most astonishing and rapid gyrations, but the three fundamental motions incessantly persist. If it be made to vibrate, as a whole, at the rate which gives any of the seven colours, the whorl belonging to that colour glows out brilliantly.*

* Adapted from *First Principles of Theosophy* by Jinarajadasa (Adyar).

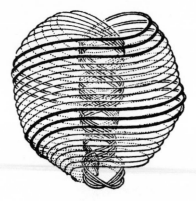

*The pulsating Anu or ultimate
Physical Atom.*

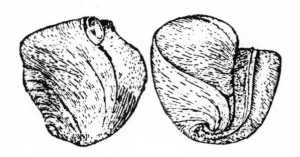

*Dissection of Heart muscle to show
the course of the fibres.*

The similarity of the anu to the human heart is reinforced by the structure of the heart itself, which shows a spiralling system of fibres of connective tissue not unlike the whorls described above. C.W. Leadbeater was able to observe the combinations of anu which go to make up the various elements.

The drawing overleaf shows the arrangements of an anu in the nitrogen atom. Nitrogen, of course, is found in proteins and is indispensable to life. We also see the oxygen atom which contains anu in a spiral. Later Leadbeater was able to observe prana globules attached to the oxygen atom. Hydrogen, not shown, has eighteen anu forming two triangles of motion, which are interlaced.

Fascinating as the subject of occult chemistry is, it is not very relevant here. But in studying the structure of the anu we are able to look at some occult postulates now more clearly:

1. The Divine Life, or spirit, fills all things.
2. Matter is an illusion.
3. Each entity, from the ultimate atom or anu, right up to a planetary Logos and Solar Logos is made after a similar pattern and this includes man himself.

A study of the spirillae of the anu shows the above postulates to be true.

Nitrogen

Nitrogen is as precious to the human body as oxygen. It is the material that makes proteins differ from other foods. Fats and carbohydrates can, in an emergency, be almost dispensed with, but protein is life-giving, and without it malnutrition quickly sets in. It is nitrogen that makes the protein so very different to other foods.

Now, it is a teaching of current biology that man cannot obtain nitrogen for the construction of his own body proteins by any means except through the protein that he eats, whether this be in the almost solid concentration of meat and fish, or in the lesser concentrations of protein found in fruit, cereals and vegetables. All nitrogen, says orthodoxy, must come from diet. This is mainly true. But it does seem an extraordinary lapse, on

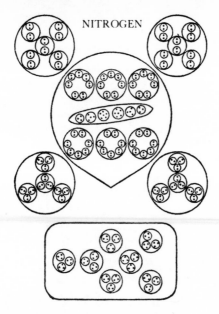

NITROGEN

the part of nature or of the gods, to have created man with a huge capacity for taking in air, which, as we have seen, is four-fifths nitrogen, and then not to have made this precious material available to the body for the building of its own muscles and other tissues of a proteinous nature.

It is a teaching, previously made only available to initiates, that, in certain circumstances, which can be increasingly controlled, the human body CAN fix nitrogen for its own use, from the air it breathes. It is taught that man is omni-potential.

The Seven Planes
He (the Logos) coils great lengths of spirals of the first order into larger loops still, with seven spirals making one 'spiral of the second order'; lengths of spirals of the second order are similarly twisted and held as 'spirals of the third order', and so on.

These energies of each order of spirals come from the materials/energy of the SEVEN planes:

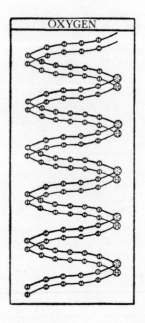

THE OXYGEN MOLECULE showing vitality globules linked to the double helix (on the right).

THE SPIRILLAE.

ADI	....	
LOGOIC	....	First spirillae
ATMIC	....	Second spirillae
BUDDHIC	....	Third spirillae
MANASIC	....	Higher Mental

.... Fourth spirillae

Lower Mental

ASTRAL	....	Fifth spirillae
PHYSICAL	....	Sixth spirillae

or, counting from below upwards, the Logoic becomes the sixth spirillae, the Atmic the fifth, etc. Thus in every physical form from the smallest anu to the galaxy, spirit is represented as the first spirilla, and we say that in everything there is divine essence.

When we become ONE with all things we identify with that which is common to all things, spiritual essence of the first spirilla. Our mental bodies lack anu with spirillae of both the sixth and seventh order; they are wrought out of spirillae of first to fifth orders.

3
Cosmic Consciousness

Those who meditate for world causes are asked to visualize the fifth spirillae of all things and energize it, for this is the target of the Logos. Its enlivenment lies behind the driving force of evolution. A man's task is to help with the evolution, not only of his own kingdom, but that of lower ones as well.

The fifth Root Race, and especially our subrace, the fifth, has the best opportunity to act on the fifth spirillae. In fact the fifth root race is an energy pattern of the fifth spirilla of a massive entity.

The understanding of man's inner nature is difficult. We do not possess bodies of ATMA, BUDDHI and MANAS in the same sense as we have spoken of those of the lower triad. But in each triad of personality there is carried vast numbers of anu with spirillae of the highest orders (above five), according to the degree of spirituality. These are in constant rapport with the spiritual essence of the higher planes.

On the higher planes we are all building a causal body of the highest orders of anu. It takes many years in hundreds of lives to complete and when it is complete our total consciousness resides there. In this causal body resides the soul of man. Its links with the lower triad are through the spirillae of the first to fifth order in the personality and we call this link the antakarana. The link grows with spiritual increase. As we progress spiritually, the causal body strengthens its links with the lower triad. The soul begins to take an interest in the personality.

But the truth is that the lower triad is but a shadow of the inner being. It is a shadow that becomes activated, and has a

Higher Mental and Spiritual Bodies

Astral Body (Emotional)

Physical Body

Etheric Body (Surround)

life of its own which we call the personality. It is transient, corruptible, tarnishable and UNREAL. Its dimensions are few but it IS an instrument for the soul to come to grips with matter and to learn to dominate material things, i.e. to control the unreal.

The causal body is really a group of tiny solar angels who gather about them substance of a high order and form a miniature sun. It is the Mansion of the Son of the real sun ... not the visible sun but the heart of the sun and the central spiritual sun which lie behind the visible disc.

Each one of us has this miniature sun within or above him ...

A replica of the true sun
A son of the Father
A spark of the flame divine
The soul
The Fire within us
Spiritual Fire or Fohat.

Our consciousness here on earth is but a fragment of that huge consciousness which we call COSMIC which lies within each of us. Paracelsus and many others proclaimed that man is a solar system in miniature and he meant it. Our personality images are but tiny satellites to that central sun.

That fragment becomes obsessed with the personality and the material world on to which it is projected. It is but a shadow of that central sun. We are only part awake. We think we are the shadow. Compare any of the shadows which you cast with your own nature and you will have an analogy.

We think we are the shadow because the material world pulls us towards it.

Again and again, great minds have warned us of this, in the Old Testament and the New ...

AWAKE THOU THAT SLEEPEST AND ARISE FROM THE DEAD AND CHRIST (the Sun within you) SHALL GIVE YOU LIGHT.

This is the real meaning of the resurrection ... it refers to the time when all men will be aware of their inner natures, and that the world is an illusion or MAYA.

'Each one of us has this miniature sun within or above us ...'

What is Maya?

Some expert opinions on the subject will illuminate us and then the great analogy of Plato should convince us that these propositions are true.

The dense physical forms are an illusion because they are due to the reaction of the eye to those forces about which we have been speaking. Etheric vision, or the power to see energy-substance, is true vision for the human being, just as the etheric is the true form. But until the race is evolved further, the eye is aware of, and responds to the heavier vibrations only. Gradually it will shake itself free from the lower and coarser reactions, and become a true organ of vision.

It might be of interest here to remember the occult fact that as the atoms in the physical body of the human being pursue their evolution, they pass on and on to ever better forms, and eventually find their place within the eye, first of animals and then of man. This is the highest dense form into which they are built, and marks the consummation of the atom of DENSE matter.* Occultly understood, the eye is formed through the interplay of certain streams of force, of which there are three in the animal, and five in the human being. By their conjunction and interaction, they form what is called 'the triple opening' or the 'fivefold door' out of which the animal soul or the human spirit can 'look out upon the world illusion.'

The final reason why the spheroidal true form of everything is apparently not seen on the planet can only at this stage be expressed through a quotation from an old esoteric manuscript in the Master's archives:

> The vision of the higher sphere is hidden in the destiny of the fourth form of substance. The eye looks downwards and, behold the atom disappears from view. The eye looks sideways and the dimensions merge, and again the atom disappears.
>
> Outward it looks but sees the atom out of all proportion. When the eye negates the downward vision, and sees all from within outwards, the sphere again will be seen.

---

* It is significant that the ultimate form thus used, the human eye, is spheroidal and takes energy in through one pole and gives it out through the other.

Maya and Illusion

The following quotations are taken from *The Secret Doctrine* by H.P. Blavatsky:

> Man may escape the sufferings of rebirths and even the false bliss of Devachan, by obtaining Wisdom and Knowledge, which alone can dispel the fruits of Illusion and Ignorance. (Vol. 1, p. 39).

> Maya or illusion is an element which enters into all finite things, for everything that exists has only a relative, not an absolute, reality, since the appearance which the hidden noumenon assumes for any observer depends upon his power of cognition. To the untrained eye of the savage, a painting is at first an unmeaning confusion of streaks and daubs of colour, while an educated eye sees instantly a face or landscape. Nothing is permanent except the one hidden absolute existence which contains in itself the noumena of all realities. The existences belong to every plane of being, up to the highest Dhyan-Chohans and are, in degree, of the nature of shadows cast by a magic lantern on a colourless screen; but all things are relatively real, for the cogniser is also a reflection, and the things cognised are therefore as real to him as himself. Whatever reality things possess must be looked for in them before or after they have passed like a flash through the material world; but we cannot cognise any such existence directly, so long as we have sense instruments which bring only material existence into the field of our consciousness. Whatever plane our consciousness may be acting in, both we and the things belonging in that plane are, for the time being, our only realities. As we rise in the scale of development we perceive that during the stages through which we have passed we mistook shadows for realities. As we rise in the scale of development we perceive that during the stages through which we have passed we mistook shadows for realities, and the upward progress of the ego, is a series of progressive awakenings, each advance bringing with it the idea that now, at last, we have reached 'reality'; but only when we shall have reached the absolute Consciousness, and blended our own with it, shall we be free from the delusions produced by Maya.
>
> ibid.

The impalpable atoms of gold scattered through a ton of auriferous quartz may be imperceptible to the naked eye of the miner, yet he knows that they are not only present there but that they alone give

his quartz any appreciable value; and this relation of the gold to quartz may faintly shadow forth that of the noumen to the phenomenon. But the miner knows what the gold will look like when extracted from the quartz, whereas the common mortal can form no conception of the reality of things separated from the Maya which veils them, and in which they are hidden. Alone the Initiate, rich with the lore acquired by numberless generations of his predecessors, directs the 'Eve of Dangma' towards the essence of things in which no Maya can have any influence.

ibid. p.45

A Common Theme

The similarity between the description of Plato's cave and the image which shackled man's views on the cave wall and descriptions taken from *The Secret Doctrine*, the writings of Gurdjieff and Ouspensky, and of the Tibetan, the Master D.K., and a host of others are striking. H.P. Blavatsky talks of shades cast by a magic lantern (*The Secret Doctrine* I, pp. 39-40) and of the reflected light of the moon on the waters of the earth (*The Secret Doctrine* I, p. 237) and Ouspensky of the reflections on a lake seen by beings of lower dimensional perception.

Just as milliards of bright sparks dance on the waters of the ocean above which one and the same moon is shining, so our evanescent personalities, the illusive envelopes of the immortal monadego, twinkle and dance on the waves of Maya. They last and appear, as the thousands of sparks produced by the moonbeams, only so long as the Queen of the Night radiates her lustre on the running waters of life: the period of a Manvantara; and then they disappear, the beams (Symbols of our eternal Spiritual Egos) alone surviving, re-merged in, and being, as they were before, one with the Mother-Source.

Commentary on Stanza VII, *The Secret Doctrine*, I, p. 237

Plato's Cave

One of the simplest subjects to meditate upon and one which is illustrative of the technique here indicated is the cave described by Plato in his *Republic*. The topic is one which will reveal unending enlightenment when meditated upon. The following is the descriptive text and opposite is the illustration of the cave.

I want you to go on to picture the enlightenment or ignorance of our human conditions somewhat as follows: Imagine an underground chamber, like a cave with an entrance open to the daylight and running a long way underground. In this chamber ther are men who have been prisoners there since they were children, their legs and necks being so fastened that they can only look straight ahead of them and cannot turn their heads. Behind them and above them a fire is buring, and between the fire and prisoners runs a road, in front of which a curtain-wall has been built, like the screen at puppet shows between the operators and their audience, above which they show their puppets. Imagine further that there are men carrying all sorts of gear along behind the curtain-wall, including figures of men and animals made of wood and stone and other materials, and that some of these men, as is natural, are talking and some are not.

An odd picture, and an odd sort of prisoner. They are drawn from life. For tell me, do you think our prisoners could see anything of themselves or their fellows except shadows thrown by the fire on the wall of the cave opposite them? How could they see anything else if they were prevented from moving their heads all their lives? And would they see anything more of the objects carried along the road? Of course not. Then if they were able to talk to each other, would they not assume that the shadows they saw were real things? Inevitably. And if the wall of their prison opposite them reflected sound, don't you think that they would suppose, whenever one of the passers-by on the road spoke, that the voice belonged to the shadow passing before them? They would be bound to think so.

And so they would believe that the shadows of the objects we mentioned were in all respects real. Then think what would naturally happen to them it they were released from their bonds and cured of their delusions. Suppose one of them were let loose, and suddenly compelled to stand up and turn his head and look and walk towards the fire; all these actions would be painful and he would be too dazzled to see properly the objects of which he used to see the shadows. So if he was told that what he used to see was mere illusion and that he was now nearer reality and seeing more correctly, because he was turned towards objects that were more real, and if on top of that he were compelled to say what each of the passing objects was when it was pointed out to him, don't you think he would be at a loss, and think that what he used to see was more real than the objects now being pointed out to him? And if he were made to look directly at the light of the fire, it would hurt his eyes and he would turn back and take refuge in the things which he could see, which he would think really far clearer than the things being shown to him.

And if he were forcibly dragged up the steep and rocky ascent and not let go until he had been dragged out into the sunlight, the process would be a painful one, to which he would much object, and when he emerged into the light his eyes would be so overwhelmed by the brightness of it, that he wouldn't be able to see a single one of the things he was now told were real. Certainly not at first. He would need to grow accustomed to the light before he could see things in the world outside the cave. First he would find it easier to look at shadows, next at the reflections of men and other objects in water, and later on at the objects themselves. After that he would find it easier to observe the heavenly bodies and the sky at night than by day, and to look at the light of the moon and the stars, rather than at the sun and its light. The thing he would be able to do last would be to look directly at the sun, and observe its nature without using reflections in water or any other medium, but just as it is.

Later on he would come to the conclusion that it is the sun that produced the changing seasons and years, and controls everything in the visible world, and is in a sense responsible for everything that he and his fellow-prisoners used to see. And when he thought of his first home and what passed for wisdom there, and of his fellow-prisoners, don't you think he would congratulate himself on his good fortune and be sorry for them? Very much so.

There was probably a certain amount of honour and glory to be won among the prisoners, and prizes for keen-sightedness for anyone who could remember the order of sequence among the passing shadows and so be best able to predict their future appearances. Will our released prisoner hanker after prizes or envy his power to honour? Won't he be more likely to feel, as Homer says, that he would far rather be 'a serf in the house of some landless man' or indeed anything else in the world, than live and think as they do? Yes, he would prefer anything to a life like theirs. Then what do you think would happen if he went back to sit in his old seat in the cave? Wouldn't his eyes be blinded by the darkness because he had come in suddenly out of the day-light? And if he had to discriminate between the shadows, in competition with the other prisoners, while he was still blinded and before his eyes got used to the darkness ... a process that might take some time ... wouldn't he be likely to make a fool of himself? And they would say that his visit to the upper world had ruined his sight, and that the ascent was not worth even attempting. And if anyone tried to release them and lead them up, they would kill him if they could lay hands on him.

Now this simile must be connected, throughout, with what preceded it. The visible realm corresponds to the prison and the light of the fire in the prison to the power of the sun. And you won't go wrong if you connect the ascent into the upper world and the sight of the objects there with the upward progress of the mind into the intelligible realm ... that's my guess which is what you are anxious to hear. The truth of the matter is, after all, known only to God. But in my opinion for what it is worth, the final thing to be perceived in the intelligible realm, and perceived only with difficulty, is the absolute form of Good; once seen, it is inferred to be responsible for everything right and good, producing in the visible realm light and the source of light, and being, in the intelligible realm itself, controlling source of reality and intelligence. And anyone who is going to act rationally either in public or in private must perceive it.

You will perhaps also agree with me that it won't be surprising if those who get so far are unwilling to return to mundane affairs, and if their minds long to remain among higher things. That's what we should expect if our simile is to be trusted. Nor will you think it strange that anyone who descends from contemplation of the divine to the imperfection of human life should blunder and make a fool of himself, if, while still blinded and unaccustomed to the surrounding darkness, he's forcibly put on trial in the law-courts of elsewhere about the images of justice and their shadows, and made to dispute about the conception of justice held by men who have never seen absolute justice. But anyone with any sense, will remember that the eyes may be unsighted in two ways, by a transition either from light to darkness or from darkness to light, and that the same distinction applies to the mind. So when he sees a mind confused and unable to see clearly he will not laugh without thinking, but will ask himself whether it has come from a clearer world and is confused by the unaccustomed darkness, or whether it is dazzled by the stronger light of the clearer world to which it has escaped from its previous ignorance.

Summary

It is against this framework that we have to consider the true nature of THE THIRD EYE ...

1. That matter is an emptiness.
2. That the world about us is MAYA, an illusion.
3. That all is energy.
4. That time is flexible, the interpretation of its passage being decided by states of consciousness which change, as in meditation.
5. Our sensory equipment is defective, or at the best, unreliable. We are like the three blind Hindus.

On the other hand, we have much to our credit:

1. All is energy, including ourselves. We have only to change our vibratory rate to be one with that (vibratory note) of something or someone else.
2. Time is on our side ...

> 'We who know ourselves to be immortal, can be gay',
> says George Russell.
> 'The end of all Yoga is immortality', said another
> great philosopher.

3. We are but spiritual embryos. Our potential is immense. The human brain alone is a billion dollar computer which lies perfectly maintained, but almost silent. If all the wealth of the world and every single scientist were wholly employed in the construction of a mechanical replica of the human brain, there would be little hope of its completion in the forseeable future. Yet we contain such a computer within our crania. And our potential in higher structures of matter, in our subtle bodies, is even more complex.
4. We have powers latent within us. They show everywhere in the huge variety of paranormal phenomena witnessed as ESP on all sides in the outer world. The potential for them lies within every man. All men manifest ESP when they sleep. If we could retain consciousness whilst the physical body slept, our psychic powers could be recognized and used by us. As a soul, man possesses all these powers. In its descent into Maya, the Great Illusion, we have lost memory of our souls.

Restoration of that memory, or SELF-REMEMBRANCE, constitutes the unfoldment of THE THIRD EYE.

The soul of man is immortal, and its future is the future of a thing whose growth and splendour have no limit.

The principle which gives life dwells in us and without us, is undying and eternally beneficient, is not heard or seen or felt, but is perceived by the man who desires perception.

Each man is his own absolute law-giver, the dispenser of glory or gloom to himself; the decree-er of his life, his reward, his punishment.*

Whenever the techniques elaborated in the next part of this book appear to be reaping no reward, or are slow in coming, then come back to these four aspects of our potential and reaffirm them to yourself. Re-appraise also the five negative aspects which precede these. They are equally important. Remember that embryos, especially spiritual ones, need constant and persistent energization at all levels, in order to develop fully and rapidly. Remember also that you cannot ripen an apple with a blow lamp! It takes time.

* *Idyll of the White Lotus.*

Part Two
THE PHYSICAL MECHANISMS OF THE THIRD EYE

Virgin Taming a Unicorn, Alchemical drawing.

4
Etheric Vision

The Third eye ... this enigmatical organ has a universal mythological history. It is the eye of Horus, of Egyptian mysticism; it is the straight poised snake of the Caduceus; it is the horn of the Unicorn; it is the biblical eye of 'if thine eye be single thy whole body shall be full of light'. But above all, the Third Eye is a physical organ innately acquired by all mankind whose potential operation is the right of every owner. It is an organ of inner vision of which it has been said: 'Our physical eyes look before us seeing neither past not future, but the Third Eye embraces eternity.'

Symbol of the Unicorn
The symbol of the Unicorn is particularly significant, for the white body of the animal represents the Etheric Body, the medial horn the organ of Etheric vision: the Third Eye. For reasons that will no doubt become apparent later, etheric matter is not scientifically recognized, yet its existence is constantly experienced, if not understood. An example of this is provided by the shark attacks that occurred in Durban, South Africa, some time ago. One of the victims, who had his leg amputated, later complained in hospital of acute irritation where that limb had been. Medical science can supply no plausible explanation for this phenomenon that is so often met with in war time, simply because it has as yet no knowledge of etheric matter.

Other instances of the etheric and the Third Eye (for the two are intimately connected) are always apparent; alcoholics raving in delirium tremens, which can abnormally arouse the

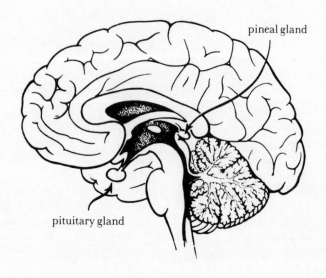

pineal gland

pituitary gland

HEMISECTED BRAIN

Figure 1

(*see Chapter Twelve*)

Third Eye, regularly reach involuting entities (Devas) on the etheric planes, and children (who up to the age of seven often manifest some activity of the Third Eye) have been known to do the same, naïvely reporting fairies and pixies.

The physical mechanism underlying the functioning of this Third Eye consists of the pineal body, pituitary and carotid glands, and vortices of etheric energy in the etheric body. Figure 1 illustrates the position of the glands ... the pineal lies between the cerebral hemispheres of the brain, while the pituitary is located approximately above the roof of the mouth near the soft palate. In operations, this gland is normally reached through the nostrils. The carotid bodies lie at the bifurcation of two large arteries that run next to the trachea (windpipe) in the neck. The importance of the glands is considerable and a section is devoted to them later.

Electric Torch Analogy
In order to emphasize and elucidate various details of this topic, reference to a simple analogy will constantly be made. The subject will be considered as an ordinary household electric torch with component batteries and their constituent charges. The three batteries are the glands, pineal, pituitary and carotid bodies. Their charges are the vortices of energy or chakras which underline them. In conclusion, a brief indication of how the torch is switched on will be proferred. This torch analogy can be carried even farther. Standing in the centre of a large room, one would, through the ordinary senses, only be aware of the vaguest outlines of its interior. This is, in fact, exactly how man stands in the world of sunlight today ... seeing but the outlines of the material universe manifesting in gaseous, liquid and solid form, and oblivious of the four subtler states of matter underlying them (see Figure 2).

But once the torch is switched on, the room reveals the most intricate details of furniture, curtains, ceiling, floor, carpets, and all the other structures not formerly apparent. The conclusion is obvious: the Third Eye's operation reveals all the underlying structures of form as manifested about us. This

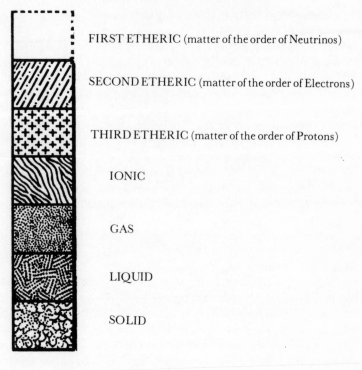

FIRST ETHERIC (matter of the order of Neutrinos)

SECOND ETHERIC (matter of the order of Electrons)

THIRD ETHERIC (matter of the order of Protons)

IONIC

GAS

LIQUID

SOLID

Figure 2

Diagram to show the various states of matter.

means that one could observe the termites in apparently solid wooden panelling; or more constructively, man's inner organs could be observed and all traces of disease in them immediately recognized, with consequent enormous benefits to medical progress.

One could materialize a thought-form ... that is, clothe a mental image in physical and etheric matter. The implications are practically unlimited. And the physical equipment is innately available to all ... for its operation, complex and involved processing is necessary, which varies in intensity in individual cases. But it is there for the development and utilization of all men who consider the sacrifices worth the very substantial rewards. Without more ado, then, we will go on to study the 'batteries' and their important 'charges'.

The charges of the hypothetical batteries are known in Theosophy as Chakras and are by nature vortices of etheric energy contained within the etheric body. It, therefore, is essential to study in some detail the etheric matter of which the etheric body is composed. And in order to understand clearly the nature of etheric matter, it is first necessary to grasp the structure of the atom, which already has attained such notoriety and whose constitution may well be studied in primary schools within 25 years. Clairvoyant investigations by Annie Besant and C.W. Leadbeater some 60 years ago revealed a number of anomalies in the contemporary scientific concept of the structure of the atom. The real nature of matter was discussed in Part One.

The atom is well likened to a minor solar system in which planets (electrons) rotate about a central sun (the nucleus). The nucleus of the atom (see figure on page 14) contains particles called protons, each having a positive charge, and around them is a corresponding number of smaller particles known as electrons, each having a negative charge. So, for instance, in an atom of sodium there are (excluding consideration of neutrons) eleven protons in the cental nucleus and eleven electrons moving about them, i.e., in an atom of sodium there are eleven positive charges and eleven negative charges and the atom is consequently electrically balanced. In

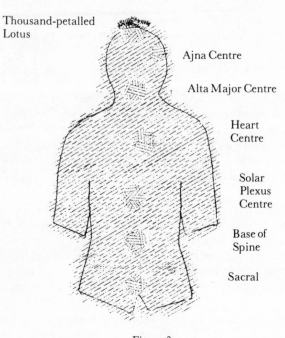

Thousand-petalled
Lotus

Ajna Centre

Alta Major Centre

Heart
Centre

Solar
Plexus
Centre

Base of
Spine

Sacral

Figure 3.

(The physical body lying in its etheric force fields)

all other elements there are different, though likewise balanced, numbers of protons and electrons. For example, the hydrogen atom has only a single proton and electron, while gold and uranium atoms have 80 or 90. It therefore is deduced that all matter is ultimately reducible to energy in motion, which corroborates an ancient Yogi teaching that symbolizes the atom as a swastika in a circle. This, incidentally, is also the Esoteric symbol of Theosophy.

Hydrogen Atom

For illustrative purposes, a hydrogen atom should now be envisaged as enlarged from its actual size of less than a millionth of an inch to the size of a cathedral. The proton in the nucleus of such an atom would be no larger than a priest and the electron no larger than a 50p coin. And the rest of the cathedral would be empty. This void then, is the composition of the atom in which man places his faith when embroiled in materialism. But on careful consideration of the emptiness of the space within the atom, the occult claim that it contains other particles not yet scientifically detected ... partly because of their 'neutral charges' and partly because of their infinitesimal size, becomes progressively more credible. Here then lies the basis of the etheric matter making up the etheric body. While the East has for thousands of years recognized those laws governing etheric matter as well as those governing gases, liquids and solids, Western science has only recently begun to handle and measure this etheric matter and has as yet no knowledge of the etheric body and the laws operating on it. Therefore, a detailed explanation of the etheric body will follow.

But first, in order to understand this more clearly, certain illustrations should be studied. An idea of the etheric body is obtained when the human frame is visualized without the gas, solid and liquid parts ... in fact, a mere cellophane-type outline minus the gases of the lungs, the liquids of the blood and lymph, the solids of the muscles and bones. Figure 3 supplies a rough indication of this. The illustration (Figure 2) depicts various states of matter. There are three physical and four etheric states of which the latter are more advanced. Of the scientific names given (neutrino, electron, proton and ion), only the first is in any way accurate, as it is as yet impossible to describe in adequate scientific language the exact nature of the other states which hold good for the hydrogen atom alone. This is because there are non-migrant states of subtle matter whose structures may be studied at some length in 'occult chemistry'. See *Occult Chemistry*, by C.W. Leadbeater and Annie Besant, which underlines all tangible elements and which are scarcely sensed by current scientific research. Nevertheless, the illustrations serve to indicate the gradations and relative subtleties of the various etheric states, and their labelling will serve to give some idea of the etheric body in topical terminology. Armed with this key, a consideration of the etheric states in descending order and their relations to the etheric body is now attempted.

The material world which we see about us and which we have come to love so much, which we hear, which we feel, which we taste *ad nauseum* is not just the gas, liquid and solid substance which we know so well.

Etheric Matter

Just as water penetrates sand in a handful of mud, and just as we know that the water, in its turn, is interpenetrated with gaseous air, so that fish are able to breathe oxygen from it, so too are these gas, liquid and solid states of matter interpenetrated by much subtler states of matter of an ethereal nature but very tangible. This very fine aether of etheric matter permeates all space and it is truly said that nature abhors a vacuum. The occult truth is that there is no such thing as a vacuum. Even the space between the planets and the sun or even that between the galaxies contains etheric matter.

This fine material flows about in life-giving streams releasing its energy to plants, animals and man alike. It is more concentrated in the region of the planets and even more so in the bodies of living things, where it forms a coherent, underlying or interpenetrating vehicle which is constantly transferring its energy to the grosser, visible structures or organs.

The densest part of this coherent etheric body is composed of charged particles which are known as ions and these are easily measured in terms of their concentration with scientific instruments. But the subtler orders of etheric matter are electrons, positrons and the host of sub-atomic particles now being uncovered by chemists.

These are less easily detected because they are mainly neutral in charge and are constantly forming and decomposing. They are naturally more concentrated in regions of the body where metabolic changes are in progress. This etheric body underlying all living things does not survive death but slowly disintegrates and returns into the etheric body of the planet itself.

This subtle body and the even subtler ones associated with it are described later. But first, what evidence is there, outside the esoteric teachings of all great religions, for its existence?

The evidence is meagre, but it is accumulating as scientific expertise and instrumentation progress, and within the next generation its existence will be accepted, even if merely as an unproven hypothesis in scientific circles.

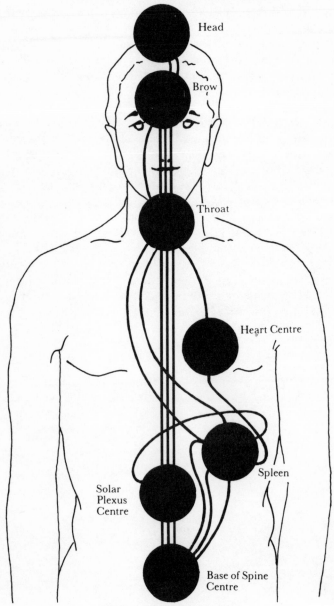

The Chakras and the Etheric Body

5

The Etheric Body

The etheric or vital body interpenetrates the family of physical shapes and extends as an aura for some distance beyond its periphery (see figure opposite). An inner aura extends an inch or so around the physical vehicle, varying a little in different parts. This body is the power supply of the system. It absorbs energy from the sun and spreads it over the nerves. It provides the 'electric current' which will give life to the telephone system of the body, which is useless without it. Food is primarily for the purpose of maintaining the chemical balance of the body and to provide heat. Our main supply of vitality comes direct from the sun and is absorbed into the etheric body through a specialized etheric organ within it. Vitality or prana is taken into it and, after it has completed its vitalizing activities, it is projected outward in straight lines from the pores of the skin. Mr Leadbeater describes it as 'bluish-white' and as 'having the appearance of being striated'. This phrase is interesting in view of the fact that, about ten years later, Dr Walter B. Kilner, of St Mary's Hospital, London, published a book entitled *The Human Aura* in which he described observations he had made of the aura (obviously the etheric body) for diagnostic purposes. Ability to see this body was induced by the use of slides made from dicyanin dyes in a solution of alcohol. Such a result is possible because, it will be realized, etheric substances are still of the physical world and, therefore, amenable to physical laws. In his book, it is interesting to note, Dr Kilner refers to what he calls the 'Inner Aura' (Mr Leadbeater calls it 'The Health Aura') and says that it is 'striated'.

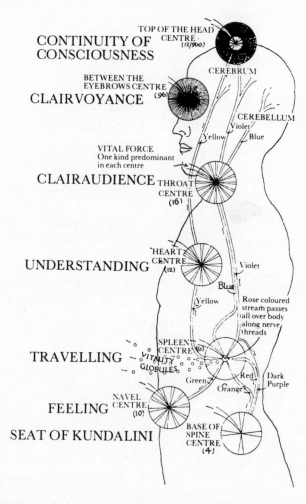

CONTINUITY OF
CONSCIOUSNESS

TOP OF THE HEAD
CENTRE
(12/960)

CEREBRUM

BETWEEN THE
EYEBROWS CENTRE
(96)

CLAIRVOYANCE

CEREBELLUM
Violet
Yellow   Blue

VITAL FORCE
One kind predominant
in each centre

CLAIRAUDIENCE   THROAT
CENTRE
(16)

UNDERSTANDING   HEART
CENTRE
(12)

Violet

Blue

Yellow   Rose coloured
stream passes
all over body
along nerve
threads

TRAVELLING   SPLEEN
CENTRE (6)
VITALITY
GLOBULES

Green   Red   Dark
Orange   Purple

NAVEL
FEELING   CENTRE
(10)

SEAT OF KUNDALINI   BASE OF
SPINE
CENTRE
(4)

*The mechanism whereby one gains impressions of the inner worlds and of physical places
a great distance away, is through the etheric centres or chakras which are shown allied to
their respective senses and psychic powers in the picture above.*
(Diagram from **The Etheric Double** *by Major A.E. Powell.*
*Note. The diagram is of special interest here because it shows the pathways of vitality
energizing the centres with the energy of prana derived mainly from breath.*

The Chakras

Within the etheric body itself, there are several force centres or etheric organs known as chakras. The existence of these chakras has been known for centuries and they are described in many occult books throughout the east, particularly in Hindu sacred writings. Six of them are indicated in the figure opposite. They arise in the etheric portion of nerve centres within the spine but terminate in circular depressions, somewhat like the flower of the convolvulus or morning-glory vine. Each one is a centre of intense activity. Two of them deal particularly with the physical body. The others are primarily links with the subtler bodies, bringing their forces to manifest in the dense material, as we shall shortly see.

All this has to be brought out into the light of day. The East with its ancient teachings has much to reveal but lacks the means of expressing the underlying truths. It is for the West to externalize the Wisdom that is hidden and to apply it in rationalized methods for the good of mankind. For instance, was vegetarian diet advocated merely because the life of animals is at stake? Is it just that? Perhaps, partly, but I don't think so. I think vegetarianism causes rather a certain increase in the sensitivity of the nervous function of the body.

We call this wisdom of the ages, the *gupta vydia* and it is perennially contributed to by the flower of mankind. Over thousands of years the great body of knowledge accumulated 'by the flowers amongst the great fields of turnips' has been carefully preserved.

Perhaps the most precious gem of ancient widsom which the West has most need of now is knowledge of the etheric body. The East has taught that direct knowledge of it can come through altered states of awareness.

In such altered states of consciousness you are able to interpret with your widely extended range of senses, other states of matter besides the gas, liquid and solid which is the humdrum make-up of your present earthly environment. In a state of etheric consciousness you would 'see' into all seven physical states. You would understand the truth underlying legends concerning the existence of fairies, pixies, gnomes and other Deva entities.

Thus underlying our physical bodies, made up as they are of gas, liquid and solids, there are existing as one single functioning entity subtle states of matter which are of the order of hydrogens, ions, electrons and neutrinos. It was also asserted that it is possible to shift your consciousness from the physical body into the functioning unit of the subtle states of matter so that you are able thereby to operate on those planes of matter and are in fact able to examine other units which exist outside of you on those planes.

Many people today are unwittingly experiencing etheric consciousness and they are describing their experiences in the full belief that they have occurred in physical consciousness. This is because in the etheric state you literally feel and see and hear with a sharpness no less pointed than on the ordinary physical plane.

An Exercise in Visualization

I would like all of you to visualize in your mind's eye, the outline of your own body, and having marked this outline clearly, I would like you to strip away the solid, liquid and gas parts of your bodies, just leaving behind the etheric part. Tear away the gases of the lungs, remove the liquids of the blood and lymph, the muscles and the bones, and let us see what is left.

I would ask you to look closely at Figure 3. You will see the outline of the physical body in shading. You should regard the firmer line as a sort of cellophane envelope or sack. A mere potential of outline. Now I want you to refer to Figure 2 and examine the head of the column depicting various states of matter. Note that there are three physical states, i.e. gas, liquid and solid. Then there are four higher states, labelled *Etheric*. Next to them is inserted scientific names reading: neutrinos, electrons, protons, and ionic.

Of these terms only the first is in any way accurate. It is impossible as yet to describe in adequate scientific language the exact nature of states 2, 3 and 4, which hold good only for the hydrogen element. This is because there are non-migrant states of subtle matter which underlie all tangible elements and which are scarcely sensed as yet by science. The structures of the latter may be studied at some length in *Occult Chemistry*.

Nevertheless, the illustrations serve to indicate the gradations and relative subtleties of the various etheric states. The labelling of these states with 'neutrinos, electrons, protons', etc., will serve the purpose of this talk, which is merely to give some idea of the etheric Body in topical nomenclature. Let us consider the etheric states in descending order and their relations to the etheric Body.

First State of Etheric Matter

It is a popular misconception that there is such a thing as a complete vacuum or anything approaching it. From the centre of the earth to the centre of the sun there exists a medium of minute particles. This medium invests and interpenetrates all that exists in the hundred old mundane elements which exist within the 'ring-pass-not' of this particular solar system. These particles are really minute whorls of energy in motion and are of the same order as 1p coins compared to the 50p coins of the cathedral mentioned earlier, but they are neutral or have no charge. We exist in the medium of what are in fact ultimate physical atoms just as fish exist in water and like fish we are least of all aware of the medium in which we live. Knowledge of this state of matter has existed right down through the ages, generally under the name of aether. Occultly we know this to be the fifth element which follows Earth, Air, Water, and Fire. It is this fifth element which will come under man's domination in this world period. The concept of aether has been held by physicists even in this century.*

The first etheric interpenetrates all and when vibrating can transmit the energy of light and heat including wavelengths not yet interpretable by human senses or by scientific instruments. It has inertia and momentum. In fact the presence of its neutrinos is only registered by the scientist through their motion and resulting momentum. Because they are neutral they are not measurable through the use of magnets. They exert

* *Ether and Reality* by Sir Oliver Lodge.

pressure and have mass.

Through this first state of etheric matter we are all linked to every other creature that lives. By means of it we are able to transfer our own impulses and energies to other entities including humans so as to influence them in some way and even to heal them by adding to or subtracting from their own energies. There is no break in the link between all living creatures. Our contact with each other depends on the degree to which each of us is able to motivate the minute particles of this plane and herein may be found the rationale of thought transference and hyponotism. Throughout the greater part of the solar system, this first etheric state of matter exists in a comparatively even and lightly packed state, but in the region of the planets it becomes more heavily concentrated, exerting pressure. The planet earth is a vortex of the substance, as are other planets, and we humans exist within a greater vortex and are ourselves vortices within the greater vortex of the planet.

Remembering how earlier we likened our bodies to cellophane sacks, we should now conceive of these outlines or sacks being packed heavily with these neutral particles so that the envelope of our bodies contains a heavier concentration of the particles than the surrounding atmosphere (see Figure 3). In a good state of health first etheric substance may be detected as standing out some half an inch beyond the enveloping reaches of the skin.

Laws governing the first Etheric assisted by certain atmospheric conditions involving sunlight and ionization of the atmosphere, cause seven of these small particles to combine into a vitality globule using the energy known as prana for their synthesis. Under certain conditions these globules are often visible to the layman. Although the particles thus enclosed are apparently identical, each one has a ray quality predominant in it. There are recognized methods known to the Yogis whereby these vitality globules may be concentrated into the body, bringing added vitality.

These vitality globules by certain means are drawn into the body-envelope to be broken down with a resulting release of their cohesive energy or prana. The seven particles now released are distributed to their corresponding force centres or chakras which exist in known parts of the body. The particles divide up according to their rays and each chakra is on a particular ray itself and therefore receives a particle on the same ray. These resulting force centres or vortices of etheric energy (chakras) are depicted on page 60. There are seven major ones and many minor ones (in the palm of the hand, for instance). These chakras of the etheric body are observable to the clairvoyant or by he who has awakened his Third Eye. They take on the colouring of their particular ray. An understanding of the seven rays and their function is indispensable to the occultist who would wield the forces of nature. In the writing of the Tibetan through his amanuensis Alice Bailey, a brilliant synthesis of the ray psychology has been made available to the West for the first time.*

While these chakras are essentially composed of etheric matter, they are linked or related to corresponding endocrine glands on the same rays. The endocrine glands form an important bodily system which, through the mechanism of hormones, maintains bodily balance in the face of activity or change of environment. An inter-action exists between these glands and the chakras, but more of this later.

Second and Third Etheric States
These two planes contain matter of the order of electrons and protons (described earlier in the cathedral analogy as priests and small coins). These particles are charged either negatively or positively and therefore differ from the first etheric. Particles of this plane have therefore greater 'ring-pass-nots' than neutrinos and are more easily detectable by science. Matter of these two planes may be found almost anywhere in the human body where cells are undergoing metabolism and also exist in concentration in the blood stream and nervous systems.

Fourth Etheric (The Ionic)
In the diagram opposite we have illustrated the sodium atom

* *A Treatise on the Seven Rays* by Alice A. Bailey.

SODIUM ATOM
(2.8.1)
[Nearest inert gas Neon]
2.8

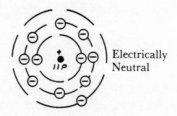

Na atom loses one electron

Ring-pass-not is greatly extended

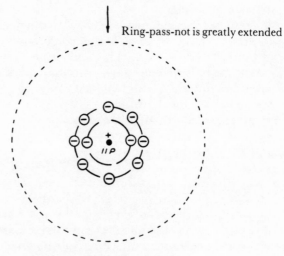

Na+ 2.8.
Loss of one electron (negative)
gives a net positive charge of one.
Becomes Na+; a sodium ION.

*The atom of sodium, in becoming ionic, packs itself less densely, i.e. it becomes subtler. It becomes part of the etheric state of matter and, with its electrical charge is **visible** to the clairvoyant or those with an opening Third Eye.*

with its positive and negative components in balance. Sodium atoms have a density which is easily measurable but when the sodium atom loses its outer single electron it goes into imbalance and becomes positively charged. It becomes an ion. As such, its ring-pass-not is enormously extended (see diagram at the bottom of the same page). It is now less dense and will pack less closely to other sodium ions because two positive particles repel. In becoming ionic the sodium atom has changed its state of matter and becomes etheric. It has become more subtle and will possess a 'radiatory' effect in attracting any stray electron for the ion is positive and the electron negative. In the same way, but using far different equipment, a plant will go into imbalance and at the flowering stage will radiate a perfume that will attract bees to it as far as the end of the garden. It increases its ring-pass-not for the same reason as does the minor life within the sodium atom as it becomes ionic.

The Pineal Gland

Some inkling of the composition of the chakras or the charge of the batteries having been acquired, a consideration of the nature of the batteries must now follow. It will be recalled that the three batteries of the analogous torch correspond to the physical pituitary, carotid and pineal glands, whose fluent interaction is indispensable to the functioning of the Third Eye. Therefore, while space here limits a brief elaboration to only one of these glands, it will be appreciated that all three must be functioning for this super vision of the Third Eye to be achieved. In the previous section it was stated that the chakras interact with certain endocrine glands on corresponding rays ... each battery, in fact, has a particular type of charge peculiar to it ... and the interaction between the chakras and the glands is consequently integral. The pituitary interacts with the brow chakra, the pineal with the head chakra and the carotids with the alta major. In the following discussion of the pineal, the close relationship between gland and chakra must be borne in mind.

The pineal gland lies between two great prominences of the brain, the cerebral hemispheres and the cerebellum. The former is considered the seat of the higher brain functions in man and has developed comparatively late ... they regulate memory, intellect, sight and hearing. These hemispheres reputedly swelled out in the skull case as man evolved. The cerebellum, on the other hand, represents the oldest part of the brain, is primarily concerned with the control of movement and remains as it does between the early and late brain parts. The pineal gland can be assumed to have developed at that transitional stage when animal-man was becoming human-man. (The occult teaching clearly states that man has always been man as a separate and distinct species, though animal-like in the early stages.) The gland resembles a recess or diverticulum in the third ventricle of the brain and Figure 1 illustrates this ventricle as a kind of cavern containing cerebro-spinal fluid. Having established then that the pineal was operating millions of years before the fore-brain evolved, some aspects of its ensuing development will now be considered in order to understand its true function.

Vestigial Organ

Occult and scientific opinion are at variance concerning the importance, development and nature of this gland. The pineal body, though found to be relatively more prominent in some early vertebrates than in man himself, is occultly known to be a remnant of the third or median eye situated in the middle of the head and which in the early days of man protruded like an antenna, long before the true eyes as we know them had developed. Science, however, claims that the gland is the remnant of a vestigial organ left over from the days of amphibia and reptiles. In normal children it is known to function and develop until the age of seven, when it starts to wither away, invariably becoming atrophied at adolescence, and the high incidence of clairvoyant young children establishes reliable correlation between the two factors.

Current scientific opinion tends to corroborate occult teachings that the gland is really endocrine in nature, as are the pituitary, thyroid and pancreas glands, for example. (An endocrine gland secretes hormones into the blood to bring about certain changes or conditions in the body: they are all physical counterparts of etheric vortices.) The latest research is establishing some correlation between sex development and schizophrenia, both of which are of immense interest to the discerning occultist. For the rest, scientific investigation has left many questions unanswered. Nothing, for instance, is yet understood about the sand-like granulations of the gland, which are described by Blavatsky, who links their presence to the activity of the brain in spheres of higher activity when large quantities of body electricity are focused in the head.

Consider the occult interpretation of the gland's functions. Haeckel's theory of the developing human embryo (now known as the Biogenetic Law), which occultism supports and even exceeds, states that the human embryo lying in the foetus during the nine-month gestation period, passes in a general way through a recapitulation of ancestral stages of man's evolution on this planet. The whole history of the human race is depicted in the developing baby as it forms in the womb of the mother. The pineal body appears about the fifth week in the embryo, indicating how early this gland began to function in the actual history of the human race.

Sex Development

The connection with sex development alluded to above becomes apparent when it is realized that the appearance of the pineal gland is closely followed in the sixth week by initial evidence of individual sex characteristics. This confirms that the corresponding development of early man sexually changed at this stage from hermaphroditism to separate sexes. And as it is known that the sexes differentiated into male and female about the time of the first sub-races of the third root race (approximately 21 million years ago) a rough estimate of the time at which the pineal body was fully functioning in man can be deduced. Blavatsky has said of the pineal: 'In the beginning every class and family of living species was hermaphrodite and objectively one-eyed. At first, the Third Eye, i.e., the pineal body, was primarily the only seeing organ. At the commencement of the third root race, the Third Eye was the only seeing organ. At the time the two physical eyes were undeveloped, but as the pineal body began to atrophy, the physical eyes developed. It now remains as the organ of "inner vision"'.

The occult teaching appears to indicate that as the physical body reaches towards final perfection and the brain develops its powers of outer intellect, the inner vision is withdrawn. However, H.P.B. stated: 'And the Third Eye, having performed its function was replaced in the course of evolution and is stored by nature for use in eons to come.' In other words, the pineal gland will in time reassert itself and emerge as an organ of higher vision capable of those supersensory powers it once possessed, in line with occult preference for cyclic (as opposed to the current scientific 'straight line') evolutionary theory.

But before the Third Eye is re-awakened, mankind has to negotiate a great period during which the intellect is unfolded and this stage can never be by-passed, for it is not conceivable to reach beyond the intellect without having first experienced it. And after the Day of Judgement in the middle of the next round, more than two-fifths of humanity will have failed to take the third initiation ... i.e. to achieve the reopening of the Third Eye, whose current degeneracy set in after the fall of man, about the time of Lemuria.

The pineal gland functioning as a sensory organ in the earliest men on the earth. It should not be confused with THE THIRD EYE of advanced man.

6
The Third Eye

It is easier to start off by saying what the Third Eye is not! It is NOT an etheric chakra though it is related to the three mentioned previously, namely:

BROW
HEAD
ALTA MAJOR

The Third Eye is NOT an endocrine gland though it is associated with both the PINEAL Gland and the PITUITARY Gland. It is, in fact, an organ that emerges with the spiritual growth of the integrated personality. It results from the interplay, radioactivity and overlapping of the three centres just mentioned.

This new vortex energy (see illustration on page 73) attracts into its whirlpool, as it were, the material of the planes of Atma-Buddhi-and-Manas to form what virtually becomes a great lens capable of psychic function. Each chakra is a battery; all must be present and charged. The, the Third Eye, the bulb, may be 'switched on'.

Whence comes the electrical energy for the batteries? The energy is threefold and spiritual in nature. It flows from the causal body which is that vehicle of consciousness housing the human soul. We know something of the qualities of these three energies as they flow into the aura of man and his lower triad. We call them ATMA, BUDDHI and MANAS. They have no form only quality, for the true nature of the soul is QUALITY.

The Antakarana

In average man, these energies hardly gain access to his personality but in spiritual man they gain access to the aura through a thread of energy, an umbilicus called the ANTAKARANA. Only in highly developed personalities, integrated and tested by initiation, can there be established a stable antakarana which can channel, with ever-increasing force, the energy of the soul into the 'batteries' or chakras.

Having already considered the three batteries and their charges in some detail, a brief discourse must conclude on how the Third Eye actually can be made to operate. From previous exposition, it will be recalled that the pineal, carotid and pituitary 'batteries' charged by the head, brow and alta major centres together form an esoteric triangle of amazing potency, whose opening and enlivening results in a powerful blending of the main energies of the three major rays of Will and Power, Love-Wisdom and Active Intelligence. And it is this opening and enlivening of the three centres (i.e. the triangle), which is done only through techniques and rigorous disciplines known to Yogis and advanced occultists, that causes the latent power of all three to manifest and be registered as blazing light. In her *Treatise on Cosmic Fire,* Alice Bailey explains:

> As these three types of energy or the vibration of these three centres begin to contact each other, a definite interplay is set up. This triple interplay forms in time a vortex or centre of force, which finds its place in the centre of the forehead and takes eventually the semblance of an eye looking out between the other two. It is the eye of inner vision, and he who has opened it can direct and control the energy of matter, see all things in the Eternal Now and therefore be in touch with causes more than with effects, read the akashic records, and see clairvoyantly. Therefore, its possessor can control the builders of low degree ... It is through the medium of this 'all-seeing eye' that the Adept can at any moment put Himself in touch with His disciples anywhere, that He can communicate with His compeers on the planet, on the polar opposite of our planet, and on the third planet which, with ours, forms a triangle; that He can, through the energy directed from it, control and direct the builders, and hold any thoughtform He may have created within his sphere of influence, and upon its intended path of service; and

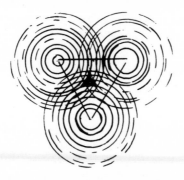

The head centre, the brow centre and the alta major centre become aroused in the disciple and they overlap each other.

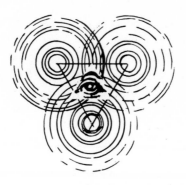

The interplay of the three head centres produces a vortex of energy which, in turn becomes the focal point for the energies of **ATMA, BUDDHI** and **MANAS.** These organize themselves into a spiritual organ of psychic reception and emission.

that through His eyes by means of directed energy currents He can stimulate His disciples or groups of men in any place at any time.

The Creative Functions

When Madame Blavatsky called the pineal gland 'the uterus of the brain', she referred not only to its diverticulate nature but to the very much higher creative faculty which spiritual man learns to develop through the opening of the THIRD EYE, centred as it is around the pineal gland. Advanced man can not only reproduce his physical likeness with chakras below the diaphragm, but can reproduce his mental and spiritual nature as a 'god in the making'.

It has been shown that man has the ability to create in a dual aspect through the sex function on the one hand, and through the mechanism of higher triad as indicated above on the other. Using his lower equipment in the creative act, man throws out a bridgehead of himself (i.e. his seed) into a fertile medium: the female ovum. If conditions are favourable, the seed will take root and flourish so that one single fertilized cell, one hundredth of an inch in diameter, will divide and multiply into the billions of cells which combine to form the human body.

A Higher Level

Man has taken millions of years to perfect such a process on this and other planets; meanwhile he has begun to develop the same creative capacity on a higher level, with here and there a human standing out from the rest whose higher equipment is ready for a different sort of creation. It is now creation on an emotional and mental level ... no longer on a physical and emotional level. And using the higher counterpart of the generative organ, the head equipment, such a man is able to project a thought-seed into a receptively fertile field and cause a flourishing of the seed into a vast replica. Thus, for instance, a seed thought in the mind of Florence Nightingale in the fertile soil of the Crimea flourished into that beautiful plant which today is called the Red Cross Movement.

In sexual reproduction, man uses the organs and chakras

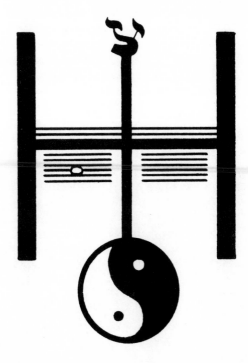

THE SYMBOL OF URANUS *which is the planet of potency best illustrates this dual creative capacity. It is the symbol of a man with his arms stretched up in heavenly appeal whilst his legs anchor him to the earth. His trunk, the horizontal bar of the symbol, represents the diaphragm, that psychically important muscular tissue that distinguishes abdominal breathing from intercostal breathing; the stimulation of chakras below the diaphragm from those* **ABOVE** *the diaphragm.*

below the diaphragm and friction is the initiatory mechanism. In the higher (spiritual) creative acts, the organs and chakras ABOVE the diaphragm are used. In practice, these are usually the various centres in the head. Again, in this higher process, the mechanism is initiated by friction or spiritual discipline and endeavour. Here, the increased creativeness leads to the opening of the Third Eye and the perfection of an instrument which can make man a creator ... a god in the making, as Pythagoras said.

Personality and Soul

A systematic appraisal of the illustration entitled *Personality and Soul* (opposite) will reveal much:

The One Flame Divine (1), which the is Solar Logos, He Himself being but a chakra in the body of an even greater Being and of Whom, a human monad (2) is but a fragment or spark. The Monad on the periphery of the Flame, on the Logoic or Divine Plane (3) between manvantaras and on the Monadic Plane (4) during a manifestation or manvantara. The Monad is the Word (5) made manifest, the Aum. 'In the beginning was the Word and the Word was with God ...'

The sutratma (6) emerges from the Monad and establishes a Higher Triad (7) on the three planes of Atma (8), Buddhi (9), and Manas (10) by appropriating a permanent atom (11) on each of the three planes. Thereafter, the energy of the Monad according to its Ray quality (12) 'feeds' its Higher Triad and the Egoic Lotus or Soul (13) begins to grow, slowly at first, more rapidly as the personality (28) becomes orientated towards it, and when the Causal Body (14) is established after individualization, and through its stimulation by more advanced Souls including the Masters Who 'live' on the same planes.

After establishment of the Higher Triad, the sutratma penetrates deeper, into the Mental (15), Astral (16) and Physical (17) planes by establishing contact with them through appropriated permanent atoms (18, 19, 20) on those planes. Materials of the subplanes of each of these, e.g., materials of the etherico-physical subplanes (21) are attracted

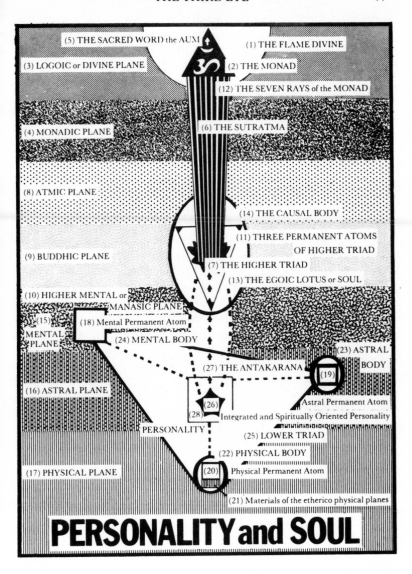

(5) THE SACRED WORD the AUM
(1) THE FLAME DIVINE
(3) LOGOIC or DIVINE PLANE
(2) THE MONAD
(12) THE SEVEN RAYS of the MONAD
(4) MONADIC PLANE
(6) THE SUTRATMA
(8) ATMIC PLANE
(14) THE CAUSAL BODY
(11) THREE PERMANENT ATOMS OF HIGHER TRIAD
(9) BUDDHIC PLANE
(7) THE HIGHER TRIAD
(13) THE EGOIC LOTUS or SOUL
(10) HIGHER MENTAL or MANASIC PLANE
(15)
MENTAL PLANE
(18) Mental Permanent Atom
(24) MENTAL BODY
(23) ASTRAL BODY
(27) THE ANTAKARANA
(19)
(16) ASTRAL PLANE
(26)
Astral Permanent Atom
(28)
Integrated and Spiritually Oriented Personality
PERSONALITY
(25) LOWER TRIAD
(22) PHYSICAL BODY
(17) PHYSICAL PLANE
(20) Physical Permanent Atom
(21) Materials of the etherico physical planes

PERSONALITY and SOUL

in each incarnation to the permanent atoms, according to the vibratory capacity of them, and slowly but progressively a physical body (22) is built.

This reaches its apotheosis in the latę Lemurian races (Zulus are remnants of them today). Later, the astral body (23) follows suit, reaching a climax of integration and activity in the Atlanteans. Orientation of consciousness towards the mental plane and the integration of a mental body (24) is the target for mankind in the present Ayran Rootrace. The personality becomes highly effective as the synthesis of all three bodies of the Lower Triad (25). The personality becomes integrated (26) and when it becomes completely under control and is dedicated to the service of the soul, the man treads the Path of Discipleship and progressively establishes a relationship with his Higher Triad through the construction of the antakarana (27) which acts as an umbilical cord for the downflow of soul energies into the aura of the disciple and for the contacting of the soul and the higher Beings of the planes of Atma, Buddhi and Manas. Through the same channel, stimulation of the petals of the egoic lotus may be effected.

Part Three
TECHNIQUES FOR OPENING THE THIRD EYE

7

The Methods of the Masters

The matter is complex because the components of the THIRD EYE are of the same material with which we must search for it. This statement is more real than apparent. Finding the THIRD EYE involves much the same problem as a man seeking for his spectacles when he is short-sighted. He needs the spectacles to find them!

Fortunately we have the teaching of those adepts who have fought their way into the Light to show us the way. We can safely use their hints and heed their admonitions so long as we have a thorough knowledge of the real structure of man.

Thus, we find that the Third Eye is NOT an endocrine gland, not the pineal or the pituitary. It is NOT a chakra or force centre as this term implies it. The Third Eye is a vortex of energy, both positive and negative, receptive or donative, formed out of the joint interplay of the radiant energies produced through the simultaneous arousal of the thousand petalled lotus, the brow centre, and the alta major centre. It is wise, during the perusal and application of the techniques outlined next, to re-examine this definition of the Third Eye.

The methods given here are safe because they are those taught by the Masters traditionally in ancient classical wisdom. But thye should be adhered to strictly. In themselves they are simple enough but the difficulty arises in that all FIVE processes outlined must be undertaken simultaneously. The techniques, in fact, require a vast change of one's way of life. But they are for the Westerner and have been practised by the author without hazard and with many rewards for over twenty years. DO NOT look for results. They will come of their own accord. Judging by results is a weakness of the materialist, he who is spiritually sick. Motivation should be along the lines of equipping yourself to become a more efficient instrument in the hands of the Masters, they who direct the inner government of the world.

The Techniques

1. The neophyte must undergo a personality change.
2. There must be a building of a channel or ANTAKARANA for the more efficient inflow of energy from the Soul, which is, in itself a unit of energy.
3. The direction of all energies of the lower vehicles and of the Soul into the head region.
4. The reconstruction of the Aura.
5. The signposts of spiritual unfoldment must be recognized and dealt with as the Third Eye opens.

Man's Personality

Man is a composite being. His gross physical body is but one of the numerous facets of his self-expression. He possesses other inner vehicles which together make up something of a 'spectrum' reflecting his true nature. It is, as it were, as if two great streams of energy had been brought together in the formation of man. One great electrode carries the energy of material manifestation; the other brings that of the world of spirit. These negative and positive forces are brought into apposition at rebirth and there is a flash of form. Man's personality results:

THE PERSONALITY
BODY

THE MENTAL BODY
THE ASTRAL BODY
THE PHYSICAL/ETHERIC BODY

The personality of man is a composite of three vehicles, which as they integrate form a fourth.

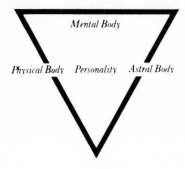

The Lower Triad out of which the Personality is synthesized. The Soul uses the Personality as a means for contacting the lower planes of the Physical, Mental and Astral worlds.

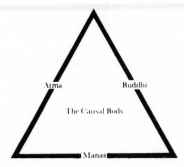

But the personality is but a reflection of the soul which, in its turn, has been formed out of three vehicles:

THE SOUL (CAUSAL)
BODY

THE MANASIC BODY
THE BUDDHIC BODY
THE ATMIC BODY

The secret of the THIRD EYE lies in the fact that we have to form elements of that organ of inner vision out of the substance and content of the planes of Atma-Buddhi-Manas. This is not possible until a bridgehead is formed between the personality

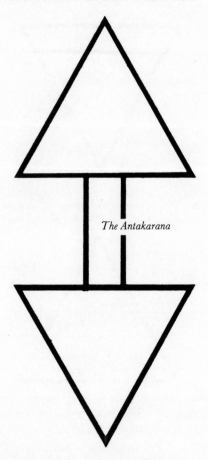

The Antakarana

The antakarana is purposefully constructed as a bridge between the upper and lower triads. It links the soul and the vehicles of the disciple who has integrated his personality and treads the Path.

vehicles and the causal body.

The link between personality and soul is called the antakarana ... the rainbow thread ... rainbow because it has many qualities which are formless but can be interpreted or 'seen' by their qualities, which correspond also to colours and sounds. Causal matter is formless but has quality. By infusing similar qualities in ourselves, mainly through meditation techniques, through serving mankind and through certain rhythms of breath, we can attract the 'matter' of the Atma-Buddhi-Manas planes into the aura. It is from this substance that both the antakarana and the THIRD EYE are formed.

The antakarana has to be built out of the atomic essence of the planes of Atma, Buddhi and Manas, i.e. out of the spirillae of the higher planes. This is what we mean when we talk about the reconstruction of the aura. To achieve this there has to be many personality changes and periods of withdrawal or pupation. The disciple must meditate (*see page* 33).

Every time we manifest Atma or Buddhi or Manas in our daily activity, we build the material of these planes into our auric egg. This growth of the permanent and enduring part of our nature, which survives death and comes with us again into rebirth, goes on slowly through the many lives we live on this planet and under what we would call the normal processes of evolution. In our last few lives, or under the stimulus of meditation, or in serving mankind (the world-saviour), or in breathing rhythmically, the process may be accelerated in what is called the 'quickening of the soul'.

The Chakras

At first, this process of induction is started by giving occult attention to certain centres or chakras. (The occultist works with the unseen forces of nature.) The chakras at first concerned are:

       THE HEART
       THE THROAT
and   THE HEAD

Co-ordination of these leads to integration of the personality ...
a very necessary and very safe step before even considering the
actual process of forming the THIRD EYE.

The process of release of energy through the antakarana
into the lower triad requires many disciplines, not the least of
which is that of orientation towards the Soul. When a
personality has three of his chakras functioning below the
diaphragm, he cannot be orientated to the higher triad. This is
seen in some examples here given diagrammatically:

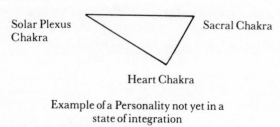

Solar Plexus   Sacral Chakra
Chakra

Heart Chakra

Example of a Personality not yet in a
state of integration

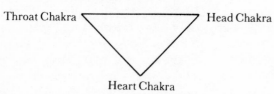

Throat Chakra   Head Chakra

Heart Chakra

Example of an integrated personality not
yet orientated to the Soul

When integration of the personality has been achieved, then
progress can be very rapid in 'soul quickening'. But first there
has to be orientation towards the pull of the soul. Many full-
blown materialists reach integration of personality but very
rarely do any go further. Occasionally one hears of a well-
known public figure suddenly withdrawing from society and
going into isolation for no apparent reason. (*See Chapter Ten*).

In these few, out of the many integrated personalities, there is
felt a revulsion for further material experience. All that the
world has to offer has been tasted, tried and ultimately rejected.
There are no new experiences offered. The material world is a
cul-de-sac. There is a desire to be isolated ... to ' COME UP

FOR BREATH' as it were. The search within produces new horizons, new direction. It is followed by a reorientation of energies that reach the chakras.

The energy of the heart chakra now flows into Ajna (the brow). That of the throat is redirected towards its 'alter ego', the Alta Major chakra. The Thousand-petalled Lotus or head chakra remains the third of the triangular target for the neophyte's attention:

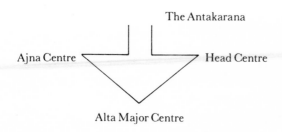

The Integrated Personality is now orientated towards the Soul. The chakras are altered. The building of the antakarana begins.

It may seem to be unlikely that a businessman, a die-hard materialist, could unfold the heart chakra but this is so. Many such individuals, in assuming responsibility, say for the running of a factory or corporation, become literally, the heart chakra of their organization. This peculiar situation stimulates heart-chakra qualities in that lotus. Frequently, the strain imposed on the fleshy heart by this discipline is too much and degeneration of blood supply to heart muscle or of nerve conduction fibres lead to heart disease in middle age. The heart chakra has, in this instance, failed to accept the added load placed upon it. But frequently, there is suitable adjustment with rapid opening up of that centre. In these instances, integration of the businessman's heart chakra is rapid and personality integration follows.

The method whereby energies of lower chakras are transferred to the higher chakras is based on energy following thought. 'Energy follows thought'. This is the basis of Yoga. We need to understand the quality of the lower chakra and that also of the higher chakra or its 'alter ego'.

Thus, we soon learn that the energies of the solar plexus chakra are 'attaching'. They bind us to the objects of our desires. This selfish love of this or that, must be transformed into the selfless love which is the predominating quality of the HEART CHAKRA. We must learn and meditate upon heart qualities and a study of the teachings of the Buddha and the Christ, in their highest sense, will give us the clues. The pictorial description of the heart chakra given below indicates something of its qualities. In our meditations we must visualize the flow of energies from the solar-plexus to the heart region. Thereafter, the energies of the heart are taken to their alter-ego, the chakra in the brow, called Ajna.

The Anahata, or Heart Cakra which has twelve petals.

The Anahata, or Heart Chakra which has twelve petals.

The flow of energies from the centre at the base of the spine, into the head chakra or Thousand-petalled Lotus is through the sounding of the sacred Word, the Aum, whilst, at the same time, practising various visual techniques. The power to visualize must be developed as a necessary part of meditation. The ability to focus the attention on what IS visualized and the accompanying action of rhythmic breathing, bring about the necessary synthesis of the three centres in the head which contribute to the opening of the Third Eye.

Summary
HEART CHAKRA – AJNA (Through study) – FOCUS
THROAT CHAKRA – ALTA MAJOR (Service to man) –
BREATH
HEAD CHAKRA – HEAD CHAKRA (Visualization) –
MEDITATION

It is through the medium of three tracts in etheric substance that the energies are transferred from chakra to chakra. These tracts are called Ida, Sushumna and Pingala in the East. In the West, their significance is symbolized by the Caduceus of Hermes.

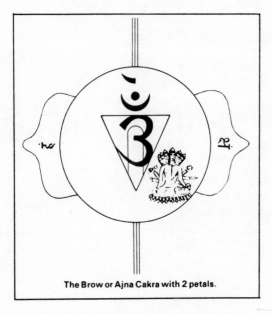

The Brow or Ajna Chakra with 2 petals.

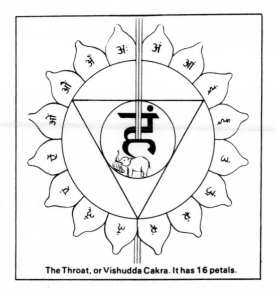

The Throat, or Vishudda Cakra. It has 16 petals.

The Throat, or Vishudda Chakra. It has 16 petals.

8

Qualities of the Soul

All the techniques described so far depend, for their main energies, upon the inflow of spiritual force through the antakarana. To maintain this flow and to increase it, the disciple must LIVE THE LIFE of a disciple. He must practise in his everyday living the qualities of the soul ... of Atma, Buddhi and Manas. Atma is divine, persistent WILL. The championing of lost causes which are, nevertheless of the highest import spiritually for the planet, is a good learning ground for the manifestation of Atma. When Atma flows into the aura, it strengthens the chakras in the head region which are related to the Rays of Will and Power.

The drawing down of Buddhi into the aura is encouraged by the practice of HARMLESSNESS in daily living; harmlessness in thought, word and deed! Non-separativeness and all-inclusiveness are other qualitites of Buddhi. Living a life of withdrawal, of pensiveness, of pupation, of being able to sit in silence and to meditate, brings down Buddhi into the chakras linked to the Love-Wisdom Rays.

Higher Manas
Previous to the Coming of the Lords of Flame, about nineteen million years ago on this planet, this energy was not known. Animal-man had reached a stage in his evolution when he would soon regress with the other anthropoids if he were not stimulated with the peculiar quality of the Venusian evolution. Consequently, there came to the earth the Lords of Flame from Venus who applied their individualizing energies to the cortex of earth man's brain. Thenceforth, the man part of animal-man

became dominant and these early individuals became capable of Higher-Manas which shows as the capacity to think in abstract terms ... an essentially human quality. Through abstract thought man is able to ponder upon matters which are completly unrelated to his basic or animal needs. The artist, the research-worker, the philosopher, the saint, are testimony to this capacity. Man is able to practise this form of expression more easily than either Atma or Buddhi. It is closely related to its lower counterpart ... lower Manas, or active intelligence. Through the practice of higher Manas or abstract thought, we build into the antakarana the substance of this plane.

Buddhi

At some time or the other we all receive flashes of awareness from this plane. Perhaps we experience these flashes as that extraordinary power of INTUITION. Intuition may only come to us several times a year but it is very real. It is as if some inner energy is released within us at the moment we perceive some aspect of the truth which forms part of the future. This discharge of spiritual fire, the energy of Buddhi helps lay down the material of that plane in the antakarana and, if other elements are present, the material of the lens of the Third Eye. Learning to perceive in new dimensions is also a manifestation of Buddhi ... the lengthening of the 'moment of perception'.

Atma

Said to be a manifestation of Divine Will and rarer even than the other two. It manifests as the persistence of such men as a Moses in the Desert of Sinai, as Captain Scott or Amundsen at the Poles, or Ghandi in the midst of his fast.

Roger Bannister, a medically qualified doctor, who was the first man to run the mile in under four minutes had this to say of his effort:

> The secret of a champion runner is MENTAL POWER; by tapping this source the champion takes more out of himself than he knew he possessed. This mental source is at the root of most great athletic performances.

By a sympathetic *rapport*, Atma manifests best through the physical body (as in Bannister); Buddhi operates through the astral body; and higher Manas reflects itself into lower Manas:

THE SOUL   .... The Personality
ATMA   .... The Physical Body
BUDDHI   .... The Astral Body
HIGHER MANAS .... Lower Manas

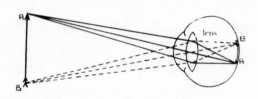

*Human eye showing how a lens focuses
an image on the retina.*

The Third Eye Needs a Lens

There is a mystery contained here. All eyes need a lens to give meaning and acuity to the light sensations. The Third Eye is not exempt and a lens is built into the aura in front of the forehead. The construction of the lens is part of the necessary disciplines that lead to accurate perception with the organ of inner vision.

The use of crystal-gazing indicates the nature of the mystery, the ball providing a focal point for the accumulation of material in the aura for the formation of a psychic lens a short distance in front of the forehead.

Astrological Implications

The astrological key to the Secret Doctrine gives us clues on how to channel the energies of ATMA-BUDDHI-MANAS into the aura so that embryonic man may grow organs of inner vision. As a spiritual entity man is still half-formed and ugly, as are all embryos but their shape heralds the glory that lies ahead

The Greek God Hermes, with the Caduceus ...

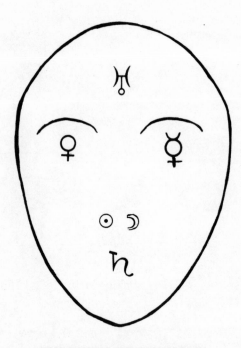

THE DIVINE PHYSIOGNOMY

As described by Madame Blavatsky with Venus as the right eye, Mercury as the left eye. The right and left nostrils are depicted as Sun and Moon or the breaths of Ha and Tha ... Hatha of Hatha Yoga.

of them ... the miracles of birth and rebirth.

There are certain organs of the body which allow the energies of ATMA-BUDDHI-MANAS to be directed purposefully towards building the lens of the THIRD EYE. These are the right and left eye, the nostrils (and breath) and the point between the eyes at the level of the forehead. They are related to ATMA-BUDDHI-MANAS through astrological correlations:

ATMA .... Centre of the Forehead
BUDDHI .... Right Eye
MANAS .... Left Eye

It should be remembered that the human face (as described by Madame Blavatsky) is derived from the Universe. Men exist everywhere in various modifications of the DIVINE human form. In the earth evolution man resulted from ANIMAL/MAN.

The ANIMAL part of man's origin derived from the slow process of evolution as almost exactly described by Darwin. The HUMAN part of man's origin came from the Universe. The remnants of this are still to be seen in the human face, the bones of the vault of the skull and the clavicles (collar bones). These bones, formed in membrane during foetal life, have been retained from man's universal inheritance. Man's face is DIVINE and carries the secret of a universal evolution which can take man anywhere in the universe, into the Fifth Kingdom of Souls.

In the act of focus as part of meditation, spiritual energies of Atma-Buddhi-Manas may be directed through the eyes and the centre of the forehead towards a space within the aura lying in front of the forehead, where a lens-like structure forms which acts in conjunction with the integrating chakras of the upper triad to produce the THIRD EYE.

The remaining correlations between the divine physiognomy and astrological symbols indicate how sound and breathing can be directed purposefully towards spiritual unfoldment.

Focusing the Astral Light

The human eyes use a lens to concentrate or focus rays of light on to a sensitive region of the retina. Here photoreceptors register light impressions in clearly defined patterns which are then conveyed through the optic nerve by electrical impulses to the brain.

Light would have no meaning to the brain unless it were first focused through the eye lenses. Similarly, average man cannot focus the ASTRAL LIGHT without the help of a lens. The lens concerned with focusing astral light is part of the THIRD EYE and has to be built by the disciple, and then trained for active use by the initiate. Until command and coordination of the lens is perfected, there will be MANY FALSE IMAGES and DISTORTIONS picked up by the uninitiate.

For instance, many perfectly honest disciples claim to have been the incarnation of St Francis of Assisi. They may well have registered, from their half-opened THIRD EYE, impressions related to that saint. It is more likely that they have served in the ashram of the Master K.H. who, in a previous life, really was himself St Francis. We are all linked to our ashrams and to the Lords of those saintly establishments. As the THIRD EYE opens, the links become stronger, especially when they have been formed during associations in previous lives. To have impressions of a previous association with St Francis does not imply that the 'seer' was once St Francis himself!

Psychedelic drugs, and other stimulants like alcohol, may also produce early and distorted opening of the THIRD EYE.

The Optic Nerves

A study of the two human eyes will soon reveal the presence of the optic nerves. These have occult significance. It has always been proposed by occultists that the human eyes have a two-way activity ... the picking up and the transmitting of energies ... those from the outer world in the energy which we call light ... and those from within which stem from the subtle vehicles. The latter ... the radiatory capacity of man ... pour out through the eyes and are the basis of the ancient proposition of the 'evil eye'. The optic nerves are the only part of the brain which is visible from the exterior. They are to be seen clearly through an opthalmoscope. It is from this region of the eye that occult

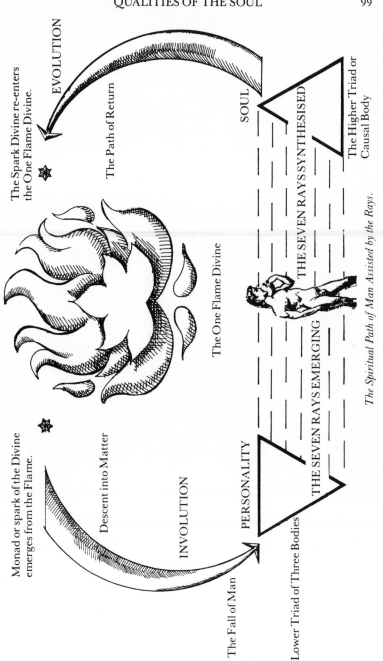

EVOLUTION

The Spark Divine re-enters the One Flame Divine.

The Path of Return

SOUL

THE SEVEN RAYS SYNTHESISED

The Higher Triad or Causal Body

The One Flame Divine

THE SEVEN RAYS EMERGING

The Spiritual Path of Man Assisted by the Rays.

Monad or spark of the Divine emerges from the Flame.

Descent into Matter

INVOLUTION

PERSONALITY

The Fall of Man

Lower Triad of Three Bodies

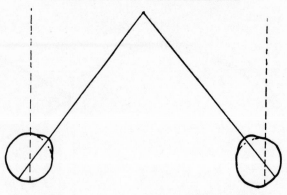

The eyes focused in reading ... the optic discs look straight ahead.

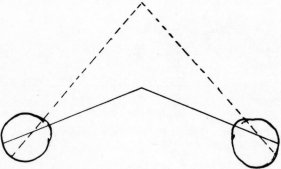

Eyes now focused on the tip of the nose ... the optic nerves are now directed to a point in front.

Radiations from the optic discs pass through the two-petalled Ajna Centre.

forces pour. In assessing these unseen and little known emanations, a Dr Oscar Brunler did valuable work some time ago. He showed that the written manuscripts, the great works of art, and sculptured pieces, carry permanently with them the radiations of the human eyes which poured over them lovingly during their creation.

Measuring in 'degrees biometric', Brunler gave an average score as 350. Rembrandt notched 638 degrees biometric:

Joshua Reynolds	586
Giotto	654
Chopin	550
Wagner	538
Charles Dickens	540
Napoleon	598
Nelson	510
Frederick the Great	657

He found that Sir Francis Bacon (640) was considerably higher than the actor Shakespeare, in whose name he is SUPPOSED (quite falsely) to have written. Michelangelo registered 689, while Leonardo da Vinci gave a reading of 725.

The outpouring of energies from the Atma-Buddhi-Manas planes via the eyes is therefore only found in highly creative men but in the meditational process and where focus of the eyes is achieved in certain ways, the outpouring can be considerable.

When we focus the eyes in reading, the optic disc or blind spot looks almost directly ahead. (*See opposite*).

When focusing the eyes on the tip of the nose, a common practice in meditation, the outpouring of the optic discs is brought to a point. (*See second drawing opposite*).

An Experiment

                      ●

Look at the + with the right eye, the left eye being covered. Move the book towards the eye from about 15 inches away. At about 9 inches away from the eye, the ● will disappear because its image is falling on the blind spot.

9

Exercise Programme

Please do not attempt any of the techniques hereinafter described without preparing your eye muscles in advance. For a full week, night and morning, exercise your eye muscles by gazing strongly at the extremes of the sockets. Safe methods are indicated in the exercise programme which follows ...

Eye Exercise
YOU CAN EXPECT TO: Exercise the eye muscles, and relieve tension in the area. These exercises are a necessary preliminary to turning the eyes inwards and upwards in the stages of the meditation. Only the eyes move; do not move the head.

Please let me repeat:

Do not attempt any of the techniques hereinafter described without preparing your eye muscles in advance. For a full week, night and morning, exercise your eye muscles by gazing strongly at the extremes of the sockets. Safe methods are indicated diagrammatically opposite.

    – STOP MOMENTARILY AT EACH POSITION

    – PERFORM 10 TIMES CLOCKWISE

    – 10 TIMES COUNTER-CLOCKWISE

The Finger Exercises
The two forefingers are held upright and extended. They should be placed at (comfortable) arm's length away from the eyes. They should be about six inches apart or may be spaced by the thumbs held at right angles to them. Concentrate on the space equi-distant between the fingers and draw them together

1. *Move eyes to extreme top of the socket.*   2. *Roll eyes to extreme right and hold one second.*

3. *Roll eyes to extreme bottom and hold one second.*   4. *Roll eyes to extreme left and hold one second.*

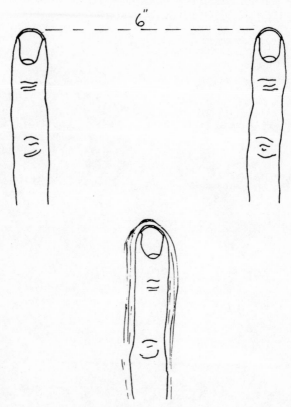

The two forefingers are held six inches apart, some ten inches in front of the eyes. The eyes are then focused to a point between them. The 'third' finger emerges.

to make ONE finger. Practise this and then see if you can visualize a third finger without the help of the other two.

ENERGY FOLLOWS THOUGHT ... this is a basic principle of occult development and in these exercises, energy of a high quality is directed to the region in front of the forehead.

The diagram opposite shows the two fingers held on a level with the eye, about eighteen inches from the forehead. The 'third finger' emerges as the eyes turn inwards on concentration.

Candles

Later, candles may be substituted for fingers. The candle flame seen as the third image has esoteric implications. It is said that 'where the blue meets the gold' the THIRD EYE may be found.

Seeing the 'third' flame is good practice for visualizing the similar structure of the THIRD EYE, which has often been described as flamelike.

The Coloured Cube

A cube of (say) 10 cms should be arranged so that each face is of a different colour. The colours should be the classical seven of the rainbow. The six used on the faces should be RED, ORANGE, YELLOW, GREEN, BLUE and VIOLET. These may be placed randomly. The seventh colour, INDIGO, has special significance and is used later.

The cube faces should be studied separately. Intense concentration on each face should be a preliminary to visualizing the colour on the opposite face. Then, the cube should be placed so that two sides can be seen at once ... and, later, their opposite two faces visualized. Finally, the three faces of a cube should be studied and then their opposites visualized.

The last exercise then should be the visualization of all the colours at once, seen as an INDIGO cube. Indigo is the colour of the Solar Logos and synthesizes all others.

Gazing at the Sun or Moon

Gaze briefly at the level sun, but never when it is high. Close the eyes and see the retinal image. Try and draw the blue towards you. Endeavour to see your own image in the midst of the blue.

(A 100 watt bulb may be used instead, or the full moon.)

New Dimensions

The ability to think, perceive and to act in new dimensions strengthens the formation of the THIRD EYE lens. The THIRD EYE is a four-dimensional organ and therefore flourishes in a situation in which *control of time* has become a developed capacity. Any sort of slowing down of time will enable activity of the THIRD EYE to become more facile.

The fourth dimension is time ...

LENGTH X BREADTH X HEIGHT X TIME

A study of the writings of Ouspensky and Rodney Collins

will reward the student interested in New Dimensions.*

One may live a lifetime of experiences in a few seconds. On the other hand, as we have seen from Priestley's experience of the birds on Godshill, time may be speeded up. This is how the real initiations of an aspirant are accomplished. It may take only a few seconds or a few minutes as the rod of initiation is applied but crowded into them are the rewards of lifetimes of experience.

Seeking the Third Eye of Others

In the way you have now been shown, gaze at the eyes of some one with whom you are in complete harmony. Try to see a third eye between the two. If the breath is used in conjunction with the synchronising act of focus, then great power over the one gazed at is soon developed.

The ability to focus on minute locations in space should enable you to see specks of dust, floating in the air. It was by this method that I first began to see vitality globules. A little later I was able to see them without much need for focus.

Crystal Gazing

There is a whole science of crystal gazing, but few understand how the process works. The clearest crystal can act as a concentrating point for the lens being built out of ATMA-BUDDHI-MANAS. Perhaps this would be better understood if I were to relate an experience I had soon after beginning to wear spectacles for the first time (at about the age of 43). During self-hypnosis, when my consciousness had been placed in the inner vehicles poised just above the physical, and when I can very frequently see the ceiling through my closed eyelids, I began to notice that, despite the fact I was NOT wearing spectacles, the lens of the spectacles could be seen. In other words, wearing a lens of some sort constantly in front of the eyes, had created a lens in higher material. Thus, persistent gazing at a very pure lens or crystal helps attract material of

* *A New Model of the Universe*, Ouspensky.
* *The Theory of Celestial Influence*, Rodney Collins.

subtler planes to simulate the same shape, AND CLARITY. Hence the necessity for a very clear and perfectly spherical crystal.

All the exercises described above have their applications to crystal gazing and should be repeated using a crystal wherever possible.

Redirection of Chakra Energy
(The Royal Song of Sahasrara)

The spiritual evolution of man, which brings unfoldment of the THIRD EYE can be a long process involving many lives or it may be greatly shortened by undertaking esoteric disciplines which lead the chela to the gates of initiation and the short run of some twelve lives during which there is rapid unfoldment of chakras ABOVE the diaphragm. Energy of centres below the diaphragm are directed to their higher alter egos in the following way:

BASE OF THE SPINE	.... HEAD CHAKRA
SACRAL CHAKRA	.... THROAT CHAKRA
SOLAR PLEXUS CHAKRA	.... HEART CHAKRA
HEART CHAKRA	.... AJNA CHAKRA

THE SPLEEN CHAKRA is not active in most Westerners. It was very much so in Lemuria and Atlantis but has become dormant unless brought back into activity by unusual circumstances.

There is really a two-way approach to the problem of taking energies from below the diaphragm to higher regions. It may be achieved, by stimulation of the higher counterpart or by attrition of energies enlivening the centres below the diaphragm. The key to both is the fact that even though average man has seven chakras, ONLY FIVE OF THESE CAN BE FULLY FUNCTIONING at any time. Of these FIVE, the head chakra is always a target for spiritual unfoldment and its lower counterpart, the base of the spine or Muladara is also active in every aspirant.

Now, we have seen that unfoldment of the THIRD EYE

necessitates arousal of at least THREE chakras above the diaphragm, one of them being the HEAD CHAKRA. This really means that no one with THREE chakras functioning below the diaphragm can unfold the THIRD EYE. Thus, if someone is functioning through both his solar plexus chakra and his sacral chakra, he cannot safely expect unfoldment of higher faculties like the THIRD EYE. Lower focal points must be given up. For instance ... if the sacral chakra is kept functioning, it can only be allowed to do so with EMOTIONAL DETACHMENT ... if spiritual development is to continue. If there is EMOTIONAL emphasis, then there must be celibacy for spiritual development to proceed. This is a hard, very hard, but painfully true proposition and anyone believing otherwise is due for disappointment in terms of spiritual progress. We have, once we tread the Path, certain implacable demands to meet. We have to tear out by the roots, as H.P. Blavatsky was wont to say, the lower nature, if the gentle flower of the soul is to thrive.

The Solar Plexus Chakra
(Exercise in Attrition)
Get your motivation on to the mental plane.

   DON'T deal with things at an emotional level. Avoid becoming an emotional wastepaper basket for every passing neighbour.

   Live in the mental world ... polarize yourself to it.

Part Four
THE BURNING GROUND

10
Pangs of Rebirth

Accepted disciples strongly influenced by the First Ray of Will and Power have to struggle virtually alone to achieve initiation. If they were to be accorded the assistance and encouragement normally given to disciples polarized to the Second Ray of Love-Wisdom, then there would be no struggle for them at all. And the essence of initiation is struggle, trial and test in which the metal of the disciple's personality must survive the mounting blows of fate as karma adjusts itself; it must respond to the mystical cajoling of the audio-visual glories of the fast-unfolding inner world; it must resist the enticement of siddhis like astral projection.

Only the personality which is completely integrated, in which all three bodies ... the physical, emotional, and mental ... are fully developed and completely under the control of the ego, is able to endure, nay, even survive the application of the planetary rod (of initiation) to the head centres clustered about the third ventricle of the brain, the core of the magnetic aura. Only he who has been malleable, tempered and tested in the hall of experience is ready for the hall of initiation. Anyone less eligible would not get past even the Dweller on the Threshold, let alone survive the flash of planetary fire on the Burning Ground.

If you have never known the sickening thrill of a straight flush; if you have never paused, guilty, 'in the rank sweat of an ensemed bed', or clapped your hands to ears that would shut out the screams of scorching tank-entombed men; or, true blue, have never quelled the nausea of protesting organs with gulps of C_2OH_5; or friendless, in the great alone, has never heard the winds speak, or the earth move; or hounded by some unknown force, have not plunged deep in every glittering pool and have not emerged from all of these crying ever, 'Not this! Not this!' – then these words are not for you.

The Burning Ground is not for you, not yet; not until every call of the flesh is answered; not until every material mesh has clung to you. But, when richest in experience ... experience beyond your wildest dreams ... and when poorest in attachment to them, then comes the Burning Ground.

All Will Have Meaning

Then, Paul, three days blinded by the shaft of light; then Hiram Abiff taking the blow; then Arjuna, on the field of battle; then St Augustine, reeling before the City of God; then Lulley confronting the cancerous breast; then Socrates drinking the hemlock; then More facing the scaffold; then Swedenborg's madness and Bacon's treason; then all will have meaning. For you, the initiate, there will be the end to your cry of 'Not this!' Instead, from the cliffs of your own mind you will proclaim for all initiates to hear, 'This!' and joyfully you will tread your way back down the mountainside and take up your yoke next to your fellowman, knowing full well why you pull, what you pull, and where you pull it.

This comes to everyone. It comes when it is least expected. It comes in a life chosen for the event, and thereafter it comes in every life like a divine right. It comes in that last desperate and bitter run-in of incarnations that pins us in quick succession to the crosses of the Zodiac. It comes to us after the welter of all our experiences in many lives on earth has brought us to our knees. Armed with the self-reliance and integration of personality, which our broad, varied and intense experiences have brought us, we can survive the Burning Ground.

There is no other criterion but involvement in the whole gamut of experience which the material world has to offer, in some life or another; nothing, not even pure spirit, can evolve without it.

One does not have to be a trained occultist or a rambling mystic to come within reach of the Burning Ground: 'The lover, the madman and the poet are of imagination compact.' It is the crises survived that matter and not the ecclesiastical or commercial or social rank of the man.

Emerson exhorted the timid to search for self-reliance in experience as a precursor for self-unfoldment. Discontent, insecurity and fear all stem from lack of experience and indicate the need for self-reliance. The world cries out for he who, having fought against nature, at last learned to work with her laws.

Temptation

So many offer to give up the many vices and assume the qualities of a virtuous life without ever having experienced the temptation of such vices. The result is that when they are confronted with the real thing: temptation on the physical and later on the astral, they go down like ninepins. It is easy to say that you can give up smoking, alcohol or sex when you have never been really involved in any of them. If you were accepted in discipleship on such a basis, the chances are that with the higher sensitivity that comes from occult techniques of self-unfoldment, you would succumb to the first real temptations from these directions. It is truly said that when man treads the Path all that is 'good' and all that is 'evil' is thrown to the surface. It is much better to have faced the problems on the surface during one's probationary discipleship than to have to face them all at once when you are also engaged in exploration of the inner worlds which comes with accepted discipleship.

Give me the hardened sinner who has fought and won his battles against the blows of fate and has yet remained malleable to the rod of initiation. Rather him than the whimpering, timorous nincompoop full of his own virtuosities, afraid of truth as well as temptation, of being led astray, of death and the life hereafter. Give me someone who has fashioned his own life no matter what the result rather than he who has merely accepted what society has chosen for him. As Emerson puts it:

> We want men and women who shall renovate life and our social state, but we see that most natures are insolvent; cannot satisfy

their own wants, have an ambition out of all proportion to their practical force, and do so lean and beg, day and night, continually. Our housekeeping is mendicant; our arts, our occupations, our marriages, our religion, we have not chosen, but society has chosen for us. We are parlour soldiers. The rugged battle of fate where strength is born, we shun.

If our young men miscarry in their first enterprise, they lose all heart. If the young merchant fails, men say he is ruined. If the finest genius studies at one of our colleges, and is not installed in office it seems to his friends and to himself he is right in complaining the rest of his life. A sturdy lad ... who in turn tries all the professions, who teams it, farms it, peddles, keeps a school, preaches, edits a newspaper, goes to congress, buys a township, and so forth, in successive years, and always, like a cat, falls on his feet is worth a hundred of these city dolls. He has not one but a hundred chances.

Regret calamities if you can thereby help the sufferer; if not, attend your own work, and already the evil begins to be repaired. Our sympathy is just as base. We comfort them who weep foolishly, and sit down and cry for company, instead of imparting to them truth and health in rough electric shocks, putting them once more in communication with the soul. Welcome ever more to gods and men is the self-helping man. For him all doors are flung open.

Yea, even the door of initiation!

The world is full of men with the seed of genius but so very few of them have the phallus to implant their seed, or the courage born of experience to nurture it in the rough soil of their environment.

Guardians of the Human Race

Where are we to find prospective initiates ... the real guardians of the human race which Plato described in his *Republic*? Are they to be found only in novels like Maugham's *The Razor's Edge*? Or do we recognize them only after they are dead, like the saints of old? They are here among us now. They are sometimes known to us as Winston Churchill, who even now works actively on the inner planes to guide his beloved Britain. With the eye of occult discrimination you can pick them out ... the Ernest Hemingways, the Lawrence Oliviers ... working openly, or sometimes slaving in backwaters like the Albert Schweitzers.

Watch them searching, seeking, serving, experiencing. They follow not the self-made rules, standards and codes of men, but their self-made laws, caring not for public censure or comment.

> Such men are even now upon the earth,
> Serene amid the half-formed creatures round.
> For men begin to pass their nature's bound,
> And find new hopes and cares which fast supplant
> Their proper joys and grief; they grow too great
> For narrow creeds of right and wrong.
>
> From *Paracelsus* by Robert Browning

While I was on lecture tour in America recently I was startled to hear that yet another actor had rejected the world of material gain and had sought retreat from the turmoil of his many personality involvements. For three years Bobby Darin remained in isolation, 'finding himself' as I heard him say on television. Then he emerged once more, a calmer, more dignified and wiser person. What he went through in that period of withdrawal only we who have done the same thing can say. Strength is somehow gained from inward sources.

Cary Grant

Almost identical to this was the withdrawal and introspection of Cary Grant in the late fifties. Wealthy, successful, three times married, the youthful appearance of this ageing man does not appear to record the shocks of his eventful life. He seems to have sampled every facet of experience which this world has to offer. There must be hardly a man who would not change places with him for what he is and what he has. But apparently he too has experienced the yearning for something within and the rejection of 'Not this!' and seeks instead, 'This!'

A decade ago a London daily newspaper portrayed Mr Grant as a mystic, a man in search of ultimate truths and inner fulfilment, a thinker bent on self-completion and introspection ... haplessly ensconced, it seems, on the gaudy roundabout of show business ... one who, looking like a matured Adonis, spiced his confession of his real self with words like eternity, evolution, grain of sand, self-examination, Ghandi, Christ and

Freud. The report concludes by saying that Mr Grant belongs to some spiritual California sect and quotes him as saying: 'I don't know if I'll ever have the courage to turn entirely to metaphysical matters.'

Cary Grant, and others hovering between two kingdoms, would find consolation in the knowledge that by their experiences they have gained the certitude of metaphysical redemption.

11

The Lama's Story

The greatest sensation in occult circles for many years was caused recently by the not too convincing 'exposure' of Lobsang Rampa, author of the best selling autobiography *The Third Eye*. A completely one-sided view was expressed by the newspapers and, whilst regarding the whole matter detachedly, we feel that the other side of the question, in all fairness, should be presented to our readers. Students of the occult among us feel that the overall detail of the book is accurate though there may be some overdramatization of some descriptions.

There follow extracts from the London *Daily Mail* of 1 February 1958. After these, comes the reply which Lobsang Rampa offered to his critics. Finally, comments made by Lobsang Rampa's wife are presented. It is for the reader, with his sounder knowledge of esoteric teachings, to decide whether to form his own judgement or accept that of the layman.

The Press 'Exposure'

The man accepted by thousands as the Tibetan Lama of 'The Third Eye' has been exposed as a brilliant hoaxer. He is no Lama from Tibet. He is a plumber's son from Plymouth, Devon ... plain Mr Cyril Henry Hoskins. At his cliff-top villa near Dublin, he and his wife live as Dr and Mrs Kuan with 27-year-old Shelagh Rouse, once a gay member of West End society. She is one of his many followers who believe in his celestial and clairvoyant powers ... produced, as he has claimed, by a brain operation which gave him 'the third eye' ...

As Dr Kuan-Sou, or under his favourite alias of Dr Kuan, he reads the stars and gives advice on spiritual and health problems for a fee. His wife, who was a state registered nurse at a Richmond hospital when they married on April 13, 1940, told me: 'The book is fiction. He had tried to get a number of jobs without success. We had to have money to live, so he was persuaded to write the book. We depend on its sale for money.' Now he has been exposed as one of the biggest hoaxers of the century by a Liverpool private detective ...

The claim of Dr Kuan (Mr Cyril Hoskins) has been made in the greatest detail in his book. On the dust cover, he describes how at the age of seven he entered a Tibetan Lamasery, and the Dalai Lama decreed that his exceptional clairvoyant powers be enhanced by a surgical operation known as 'the opening of the third eye'. In the book he explains his 17-day-long ordeal which gave him his third eye ...

But he has never been to Tibet. He has never had a brain operation. He is a sick man with heart trouble and other ailments. These are some of the claims he makes: That after he left Tibet he fought with the Chinese Nationalist Forces against Japan and was taken prisoner. That after the first A-bomb dropped on Japan he escaped in a fishing boat to Korea and made his way to Britain by way of Moscow and New York. That he has flown in a flying saucer and is a son of a prince of Tibet.

These are the facts: He is 47, the son of a master-plumber, Joseph Henry Hoskins. After leaving school he helped his father until he died in 1937, then went with his mother to live in Nottinghamshire. He worked for a firm of surgical instrument manufacturers, and there became a clerk with a correspondence school of engineering. There he shaved his head, grew a beard and changed his name to Dr Kuan-Suo. Now he and his wife live with Mrs Rowse, daughter of Mr John Isherwood, paper mill owner of New Mills, Derbyshire, at Howth near Dublin.

From his sickbed, Mr Hoskins sent me a message maintaining the authenticity of the book. It said: 'This story is true, but for very special reasons the identity of the Tibetan author cannot be revealed. I have never bedraggled anyone in my life, no matter what the cost. I shall not bedraggle anyone now. I have almost no chance of life. This shock is reducing it even more. I must be guided by my conscience in what I do. My life has been hard and bitter and I consider in this other blow of publicity I am doing what is right.'

Mrs Rowse's husband, John, ex-regular Army Officer, who lives in Kensington, said at his city office last night: 'I know the stories that are circulating about Lobsang Rampa, but I believe none of them and I do not want to discuss them. I have known him for two years and I am convinced he is thoroughly genuine. He has been a guest in my home, a good friend of my wife and myself, and I am quite sure he is no phoney.'

Mrs Rowse's mother, Mrs Margaret Isherwood, told me: 'She has told me he is a brilliant surgeon and she believes implicitly that he is from a high-ranking Tibetan family. She believes he has wonderful mystic powers.'

His agent, Mr Brooks of Mayfair, said: 'I am surprised. He possesses extra-ordinary powers of telepathy. He has given me proof on a number of occasions.'

Mr F. J. Warburg, director of the firm who published the book, said: 'I am very surprised. I thought he was Chinese. We were not sure ourselves about the book and sent it to twenty different people who all gave it different opinions. In the first edition we printed a foreword in which we said we could not check the authenticity of the facts and left it to the reader to judge. It is published as a non-fiction work.'

Lobsang Rampa's Reply

The Third Eye is absolutely true and all that I write in that book is fact. I, a Tibetan Lama, now occupy what was originally the body of a Western man, and I occupy it to the permanent and total exclusion of the former occupant. He gave his willing consent, being glad to escape from life on this earth in view of my urgent need. The actual change-over occurred on the 13 June 1949, but the way had to be prepared some time before that. I know that I have a special task to do, and I became aware that it would be necessary to come to England for various reasons connected with it. In the latter part of 1947, I was able by telepathy to send impressions to a suitable person. In February 1948, he changed his name by legal Deed Poll and took the name of Kuan Suo as directed by me.

To make the change-over easier, he altered his addresses a number of times and lost contact with all friends and relatives. On the 13 June, 1949, he had a slight accident which resulted in concussion and which 'knocked him out of himself'. This enabled me to take over.

I tried very hard indeed to obtain employment in England but for various reasons there was no assistance from the Employment

Exchange. For years I visited Employment Exchanges and the Appointment Bureaux in Tavistock Square, London. I was also registered with a number of private Employment Agencies and paid quite a considerable amount to them in fees but none of them did anything for me.

For some time we lived on capital which had been saved and upon anything which I was able to earn from doing free-lance writing or advertising.

I have a special task to do because during my life in Tibet I had been to the Chang Tang Highlands where I had seen a device which enables people to see the human aura. I am clairvoyant and can see the aura as I have demonstrated to many people at many times, but I was aware that if doctors and surgeons could see the human aura then they could determine the illness afflicting a human body before it was at all serious. It was not possible for me to come to England in the body which I then had. I tried, but to no avail.

The aura is merely a corona of discharge of the body, of the life force. It is similar to the corona discharge from high tension cables which can be seen by almost anyone on a misty night, and if money would be spent on research, medical science would have one of the most potent tools for the cure of disease. I had to have money in order to carry out my own research, but I have never taken money for curing people's illnesses or for taking their troubles off their shoulders, as has been misrepresented in a certain paper.

And how did *The Third Eye* come to be written? I certainly did not want to write it but I was desperate to get a job so that I could get on with my allotted task. I tried for job after job without avail, eventually a friend offered to put me in touch with a gentleman who might be able to use my service. Mr Brooks said that I should write a book. I insisted that I did not want to write a book and so we parted. Mr Brooks wrote to me again and once more suggested that I should write a book. In the interval between seeing him and receiving his letter I had been for other interviews and had been rejected. So, with much reluctance I accepted Mr Brooks' offer to write a book, and here again I repeat that everything in that book is true. Everything said in my second book *Medical Lama* is true also. One should not place too much credence in 'experts' or 'Tibetan Scholars' when it is seen how one 'expert' contradicts the other, when they cannot agree on what is right and what is wrong, and after all, how many of those 'Tibetan Scholars' have entered a lamasery at the age of seven, and worked all the way through life as a Tibetan, and then taken over the body of a Westerner? I have!

Testimony of Sanya Kuan S.R.N.

It is an ill wind ... As far as I can see, it appears that the announcement regarding the author of *The Third Eye* has done nothing but enhance Lobsang Rampa's prestige, and resulted in bringing his best seller more than ever before the public eye. One lady, an authority on Eastern methods and religions, made the remark that if the facts were true, then Lobsang Rampa was an even greater person than ever. Now she is certain that the facts ARE true.

Many people will wonder about the one who occupied that Western body before it was taken over by a Tibetan, and I, as the wife, would like to tell something of the events leading to the change of personality.

At the first indication of something different, I was more than a little startled. We were leading a quiet life in Surrey, my husband being on the staff of a Correspondence College, in an advisory capacity, and the war had been over for two years. Out of the blue came his remark toward the end of 1947. Sitting quietly for some time, he startled me by saying, 'I am going to change my name.' I looked at him aghast for I failed to see any point in doing such a thing. We had nothing to hide, nothing from which to run away. It took me some time to recover after he continued, 'Yes, we will change our name by Deed Poll. We will call ourselves Kuan Suo'.

By February, 1948, all legal formalities had been completed and we had no further right to our previous name. My husband's employer was not pleased, but there was little he could do about it, especially as at about that time one of the firm's directors had made an alteration to his own name.

Of course, everyone thought that we had at least taken leave of our senses, but that never bothered me. I had lived with my husband for eight years and knew that if he had a hunch to do anything at all, there was a very good reason for it. Soon, however, we noticed people were not saying our name when addressing us, and even after seeing it written, they didn't seem able to spell it; for that reason we later contracted it to Ku'an. I want to clarify this point to show that we have at no time used an alias as has been mistakenly suggested.

At about this time my husband talked a great deal about the East and on occasions he did in fact wear Eastern dress; he often seemed to be very pre-occupied in his manner, and I have known him to fall into a 'trance state' and speak in an unfamiliar tongue, which I now believe to be a language of the East. In July 1948, he again made a sudden decision ... this time to give up his job. This he did to the consternation of the employer who had always found him to be a very useful and conscientious member of his staff. The idea behind this was so that we could leave the district and lose all contact, which we did. Within a year we had completely lost touch with previous acquaintances and with our former life. We managed to exist on what we had saved, together with what we could earn from various forms of writing.

The day I happened to look out of the window and see my husband lying at the foot of a tree in the garden, is something I shall never forget. I hurried out to find he was recovering, but to me, a trained nurse, he seemed to be stunned or something. When eventually he regained consciousness, he seemed to act differently and in a way I did not understand.

After getting him indoors and upstairs to our flat to rest, the main thought in my mind was to get a doctor as quickly as possible, but I was reckoning without him ... he seemed to sense my alarm, and implored me not to do so, assuring me that he was quite alright. Certainly his speech seemed different, more halting, as if he was unfamiliar with the language, and his voice appeared deeper than before.

For sometime I was quite concerned, for something seemed to have happened to his memory ... before speaking or moving he appeared to be making calculations; much later I learned that he was 'tuning in to my mind' to see what was expected of him. I do not mind admitting that in the early stages I was very worried, but now it seems quite natural. I have never ceased to wonder that such an ordinary individual as myself should be so closely associated with such a remarkable occurrence as the advent of a Tibetan Lama to the Western World.

12
The Pineal Gland

Ask most doctors to describe the pineal gland, and they will tell you that it is a small organ in the centre of the brain which in the adult human has no useful function whatever.

It very much looks as if they may be wrong. Medical scientists involved in advanced brain research are coming to the conclusion that the pineal gland might well have the most astonishing qualities ... if only we could learn to use them. It could be a 'Third Eye' ... a 'window on life' ... through which we could see a whole new dimension of consciousness, once we discover how to look through it. Some scientists think the pineal gland is our link between the 'psychical body' and the spinal nervous system of the brain, and holds the key to instinct, 'sixth sense', and other complex mysteries of the mind. The gland itself is oval-shaped and about the size of a pea. It lies between the two halves of the brain, and because it is easily accessible, surgeons have long known of its existence.

Key to Mental Power
According to an ancient Indian tradition, every human being possesses a 'Third Eye', a kind of mystical organ that provides us with a window on our spiritual life and holds the key to our mental power. Today many scientists believe that this 'Third Eye', far from being just a spiritual symbol, is in fact the pineal gland. The latest theory is that the gland forms a connecting link between man's 'psychic body' and his nervous system, and translates the subtle impressions received by the subconscious mind into signals that can be 'understood' by the brain.

These theories were ridiculed when first evolved. Today,

they do not raise as much as a smile among even the most sceptical scientists. For recent discoveries are proving that they are probably correct.

We know that many birds and animals still possess faculties which man has lost in the process of evolution, and it sometimes happens that by studying certain aspects of an animal's brain mechanism, we can arrive at a better understanding of our own. This is certainly true with the pineal gland. In several species of fish and lizard, the gland is quite large in comparison with the rest of the brain. In some cases ... the lamprey, for example ... it extends as far as the forehead, where there is a small cavity covered by a thin membrane of skin. The lamprey's pineal looks like an eye, and is linked with the brain by a thick 'optic nerve'. In fact, the gland strongly resembles an eye in just about every animal except man himself.

The human pineal no longer has anything in common with a sensory organ. It has just the normal functions of a gland ... in other words, is capable of secreting one or more substances. The human pineal is made up of two types of cells: pineocytes and astrocytes. The latter are found throughout the nervous system, but they are not present in any other *gland* in the human body. The pineal, therefore, appears to be a gland which also acts as a nerve tissue ... a situation that has given the scientist quite a headache, because theoretically it just isn't possible.

Every organ in the human body depends on something else ... nothing works entirely by itself. Even the heart, which has its own nervous system, is governed by current flowing from the nerve centres. And this presents the scientists with another problem ... for although the pineal gland is linked with the brain, it is not activated by the nerve-cells that surround it. It appears, in fact, to be activated by 'messages' that reach it from the eyes ... messages conveyed by the pupils rather than by retinal images. But whether it plays a major part in analysing these messages is something that still remains to be established. Some scientists think that the pineal gland may be more vastly important than research has so far shown.

Cosmic Ray Receiver

Experiments have proved that it has a direct influence on the thyroid gland (one of the body's main hormone producers) and it is also believed to govern a human being's emotional state. Another even more startling theory is that it acts as a kind of built-in cosmic ray receiver. Cosmic radiation is now known to exercise a considerable influence over our everyday lives, and we know, too, that many animals are unusually sensitive to it.

It may be that the pineal gland acts as a kind of regulator that adjusts the body's organism depending on the amount of cosmic radiation it receives. Whatever the truth, science is still a long way from ferreting out the pineal gland's secrets.

Other recommended books...

YOUR PSYCHIC POWERS
AND HOW TO DEVELOP THEM

Hereward Carrington Ph.D. The *only* detailed instruction manual of its kind for developing trance-mediumship! This amazing book, written by a dedicated psychical researcher, was based on notes he wrote for circulation amongst members of New York psychical societies. Introduces the whole range of psychic manifestations, including the human aura, telepathy, clairvoyance, crystal gazing, automatic writing, obsession and insanity, hypnotism and mesmerism, astral projection, spirit- and thought-photography and materialization. Guidance is also given in distinguishing between true and false phenomena. Dr Carrington maintained: ' . . . **we are all more or less mediumistic or psychic, and need only to cultivate our powers in order to develop them, and bring them to maturity.**'

SPIRITUAL HEALING
THE POWER OF THE GENTLE TOUCH

Rev. Dudley Blades. Here, perhaps for the first time, the fundamental issues raised by spiritual healing are explained in a way that everyone can understand. The author describes the mechanics of healing, sources of healing power, the aura, colour healing, reincarnation, lost souls, spirit possession, divine energy, spirit guides, and the etheric body. Techniques and practice of contact and absent healing are examined and a typical healing session is presented, with advice on how to join an already established group. This book demonstrates that healing is a craft that can be learned, for 'There is an apprenticeship to be served and a Master to serve under'.

PSYCHIC EXPERIENCE FOR YOU
HOW TO CONTROL AND USE LATENT MENTAL FACULTIES

Rodney Marsden. Psychic ability is normal, not supernatural! This book explores telepathy, clairvoyance, psychokinesis, dreams, water divining and other dowsing, divination and healing, with tests and exercises for their development. The key to making use of psychic abilities lies in a lessening of your involvement with information being fed to your brain from the 'normal' sense organs. *Other contents:* Is it mere coincidence?; How to calculate the significance level of psychic experiments; Learning to use psychic techniques; The psychic power of dreams; Psychometry — an advanced form of ESP; Towards an understanding of the psychic world.

THE TRAVELLER'S GUIDE TO THE ASTRAL PLANE

Steve Richards. For thousands of years men have believed that beyond the physical world there is another world of reality and experience. Access to this world is gained by the subtle or astral body, released from its prison of flesh. Drawing on a fascinating array of both Eastern and Western material, the author presents a unique panoramic view of astral reality — the essential features of the astral landscape, the many facets of astral experience, and how to embark upon your own never-to-be-forgotten journey of exploration beyond the body.

PSYCHIC SELF-DEFENCE

Dion Fortune. Free yourself from Psychic Attack and win back the money, love, and power that is rightfully yours! ARE YOU BEING VICTIMIZED BY A PSYCHIC ATTACK? Are you having difficulties in your private life . . . troubled by unusual nervousness . . . unable to sleep properly? These could be warning signs that you are under Psychic Attack. PSYCHIC SELF-DEFENCE IS SIMPLE AND EASY TO USE! Now, at last, you can defend yourself against all forms of Psychic Attack, with powerful techniques of PSYCHIC SELF-DEFENCE . . . move from the shadows into radiant sunlight . . . win back all the things that are rightfully yours. The author analyses hauntings, modern witchcraft, the pathology of non-human contacts, even the elusive psychic element which sometimes appears in mental illness, and, more importantly she actually spells out the methods used by sorcerers to mount a psychical attack. Safeguard *yourself* from PSYCHIC ATTACK.

PRACTICAL EGYPTIAN MAGIC

Murry Hope. This complete guide to the magical system of the ancient Egyptians describes the nature and development of Egyptian magic and provides a concise simplified version of it for the modern occultist. Murry Hope describes the principal hieroglyphs used in Egyptian occult symbolism and explains the Egyptian concept of the after-life. Information is also given on the Egyptian system of deities, their origins and esoteric meanings; Egyptian magical practices as described in THE BOOK OF THE DEAD and other sacred texts; and much more. The author dispenses with the original lengthy entombment procedures and describes simple and safe rituals based on the ancient Egyptian system.

THE SHINING PATHS

AN EXPERIENTIAL JOURNEY
THROUGH THE TREE OF LIFE

Dolores Ashcroft-Nowicki. *Illustrated.* A collection of pathworkings or visualization exercises for newcomers (though thoroughly tested by advanced students) on the Qabalistic Tree of Life. Opens the doors of inner perception! All the temples of the Tree are fully described, starting in the temple of Malkuth, the point of departure for all other paths and spheres of the Tree. A respected modern occultist, Dolores Ashcroft-Nowicki studied under the late W. E. Butler and with him was a founder-member of the Servants of the Light School of Occult Science, of which she is now Director of Studies. For hundreds of years the secret methods of pathworking have been kept strictly within occult circles but now you too can embark on the search for self-knowledge — the greatest quest of mankind.

EXPERIMENTAL MAGIC

THE OCCULT ROAD TO RICHES

Just one subject covered in EXPERIMENTAL MAGIC — a detailed compendium of occult techniques and practices with all the information necessary for you to try them out yourself. In EXPERIMENTAL MAGIC you can discover the amazing ways magicians go about the tasks of
* **Finding gold**
* **Hunting ghosts**
* **Even attempting to achieve invisibility!**
This book was written by a practising occultist with the express purpose of presenting practical occult techniques in language that a layman understands.

MAGIC FOR THE AQUARIAN AGE

A CONTEMPORARY TEXTBOOK OF
PRACTICAL MAGICAL TECHNIQUES

Marian Green. *Illustrated.* Here is a powerful book of exercises and methods for developing magical techniques that have been adapted to twentieth-century life — and that really work! There is no occult 'jargon' since the work is meant to be interesting, fun — and satisfying. Marian Green is a well-known figure in occult circles and is editor of *Quest* magazine. *Includes:* Meditation — the art of stopping time; Visualization — creating a place in infinity; Getting fit for Magic; Divination — stretching your senses; The equipment of Magic; The Rite way to work; A week of magical work.